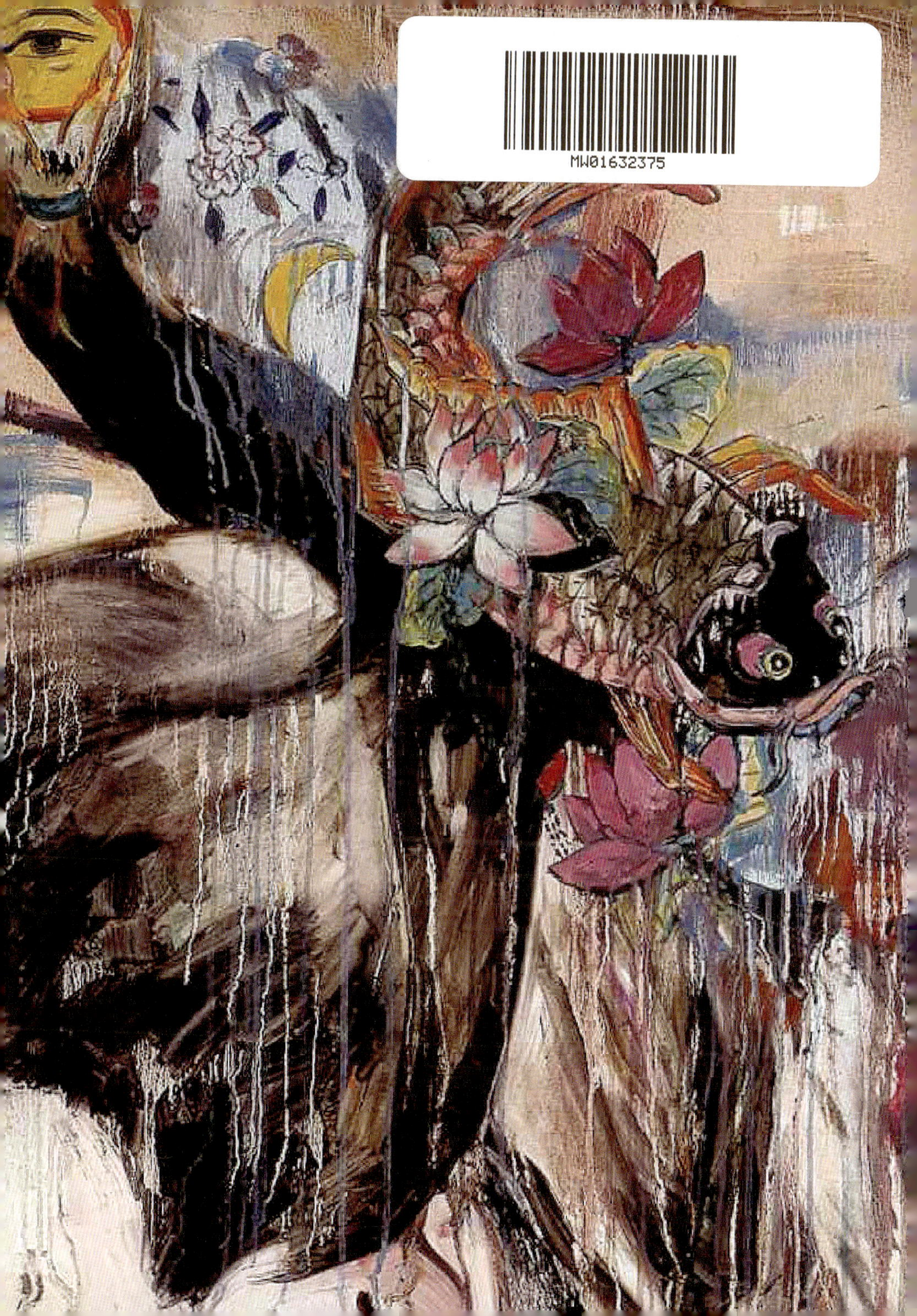
MW01632375

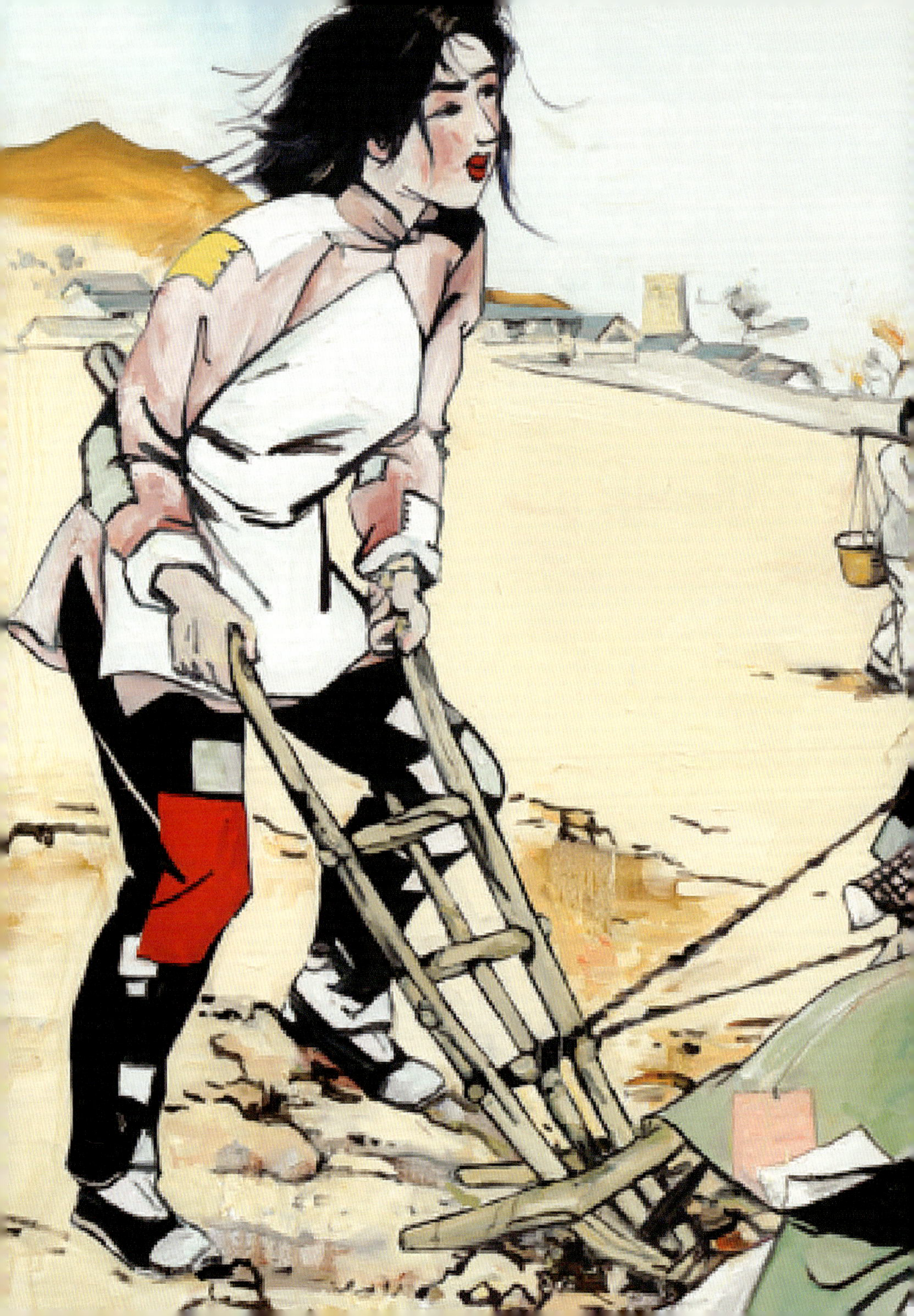

Hung Liu

Ghosts | Seventy Portraits

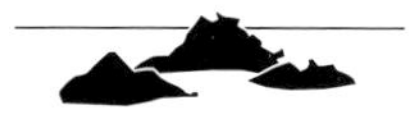

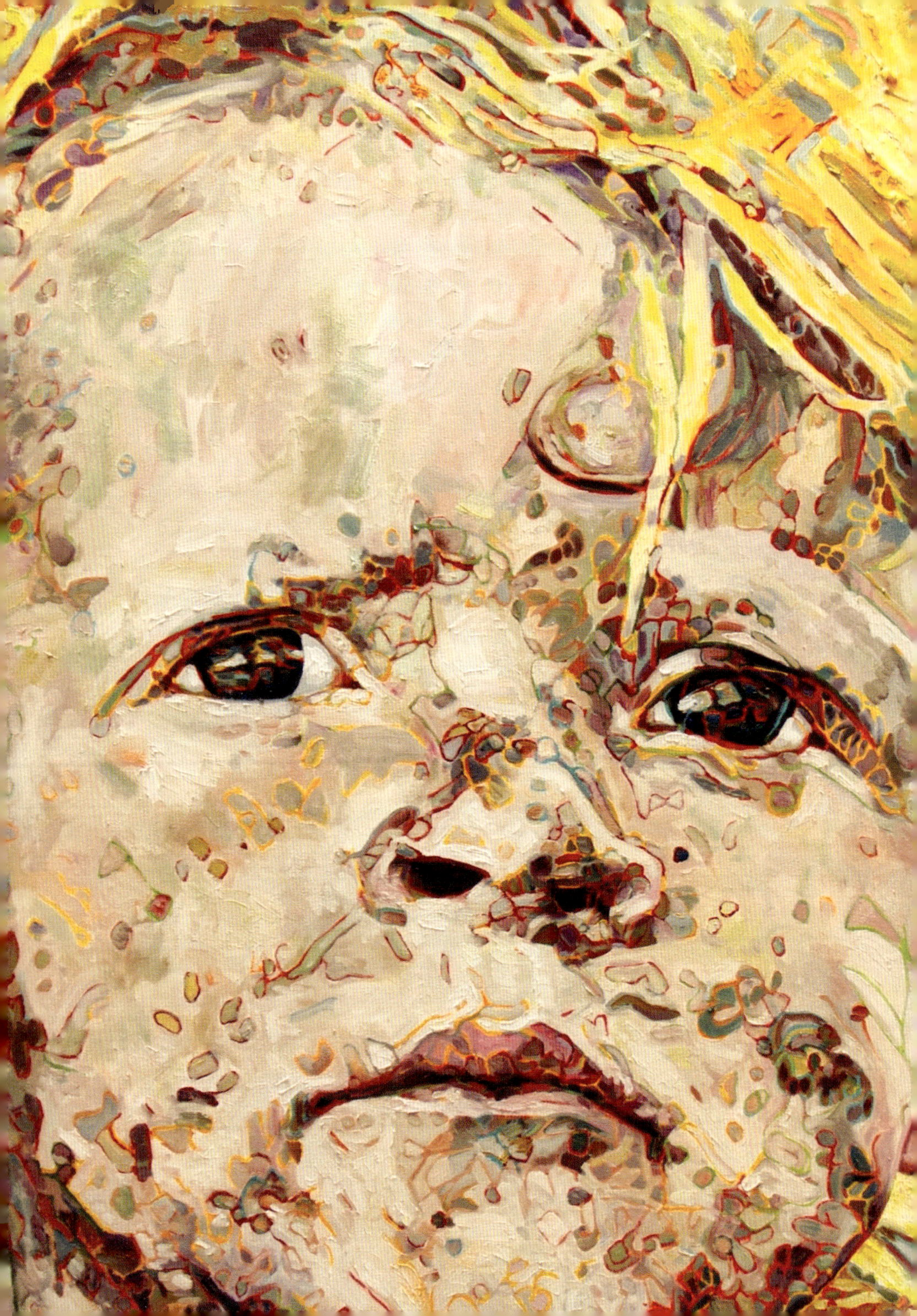

Hung Liu

Ghosts | Seventy Portraits

Edited by Bart Schneider

Kelly's Cove Press

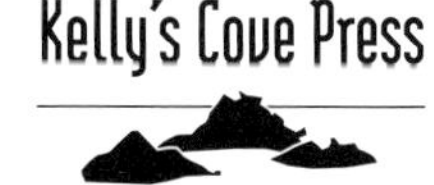

Published by Kelly's Cove Press
2733 Prince Street
Berkeley, CA 94705
www.kellyscovepress.com

Published in the United States of America

ISBN 978-0-578-72602-1

Library of Congress Control Number: 2020913116

First printing October 2020

Cover: *Cherry Lips*, 1995
oil on canvas | 84 x 60 inches | Private collection

Opening page painting: Detail from *Chinese Profile IV*, 1998
Full painting and specifications on page 23

Painting across from the half title: Detail from *The Heroines*, 2012
Full painting and specifications on pages 60–61

Painting across from the title page: Detail from *Towhead*, 2018
Full painting and specifications on page 51

Painting on page 127: Detail from *Refugee: Woman and Children*, 2000
Full painting and specifications on page 85

Painting on endpaper: Detail from *September*, 2001
Full painting and specifications on page 43

Photograph of Hung Liu on page 121 by Jeff Kelley

When I moved to the West, exactly half a lifetime ago, I carried my ghosts with me. The ghosts I carry are a burden, but also a blessing.

Cultural Relics

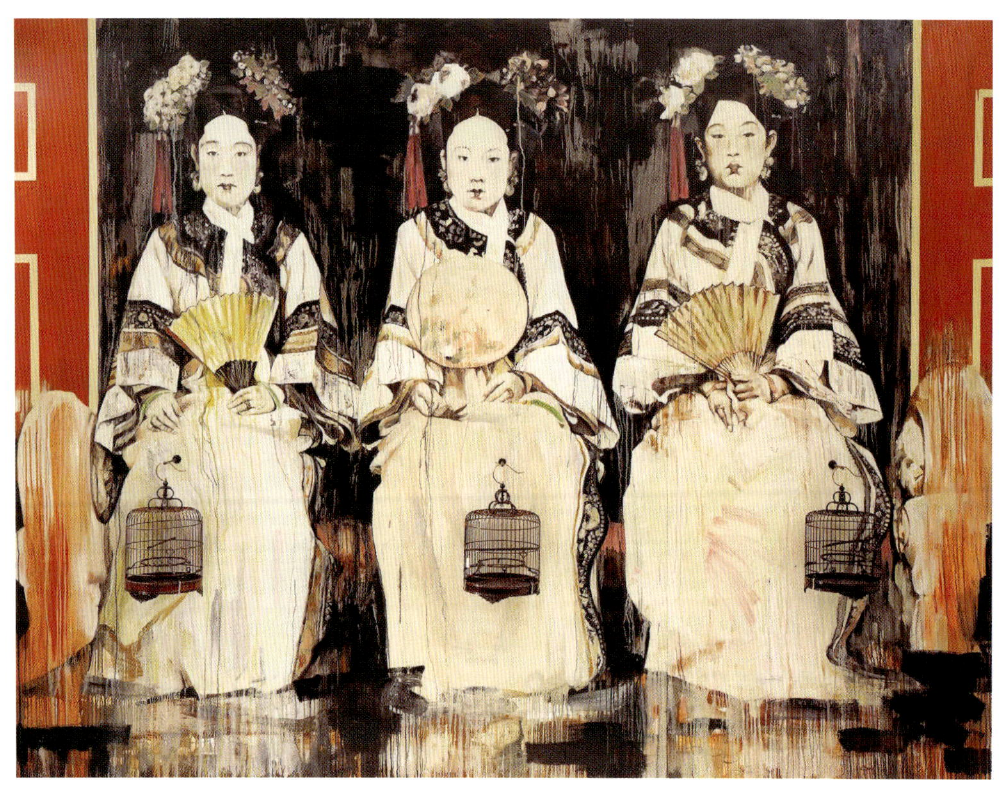

Three Fujins | 1995

oil on canvas, three bird cages | 96 x 126 x 12 inches | Private collection

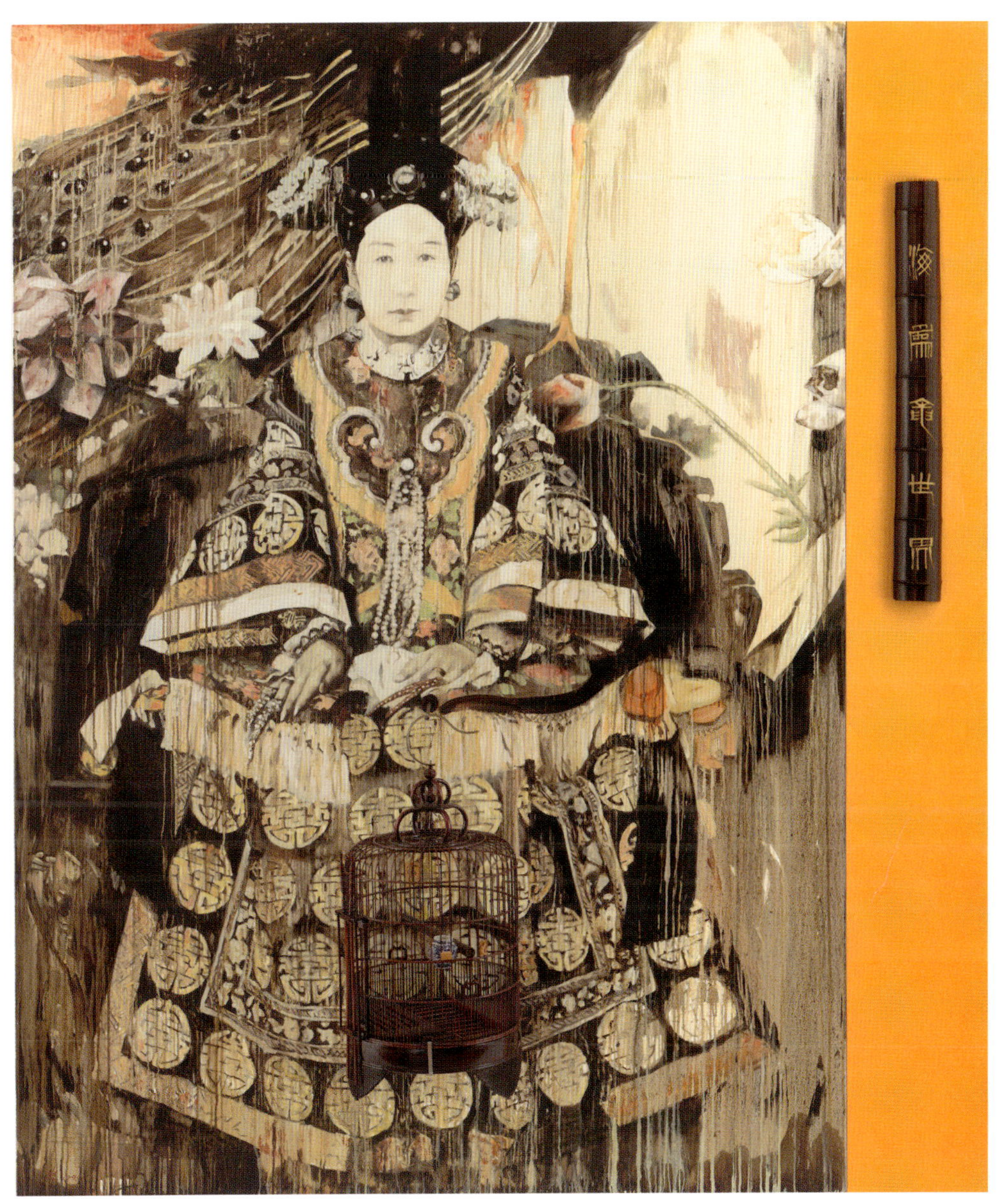

The Ocean Is the Dragon's World | 1995

oil on canvas, painted wood panel, metal rod, bird cage | 96 x 82 x 12 inches | Smithsonian American Art Museum

A Feather in One's Cap
1997–2004
oil on canvas, 96 x 120 inches
Private collection

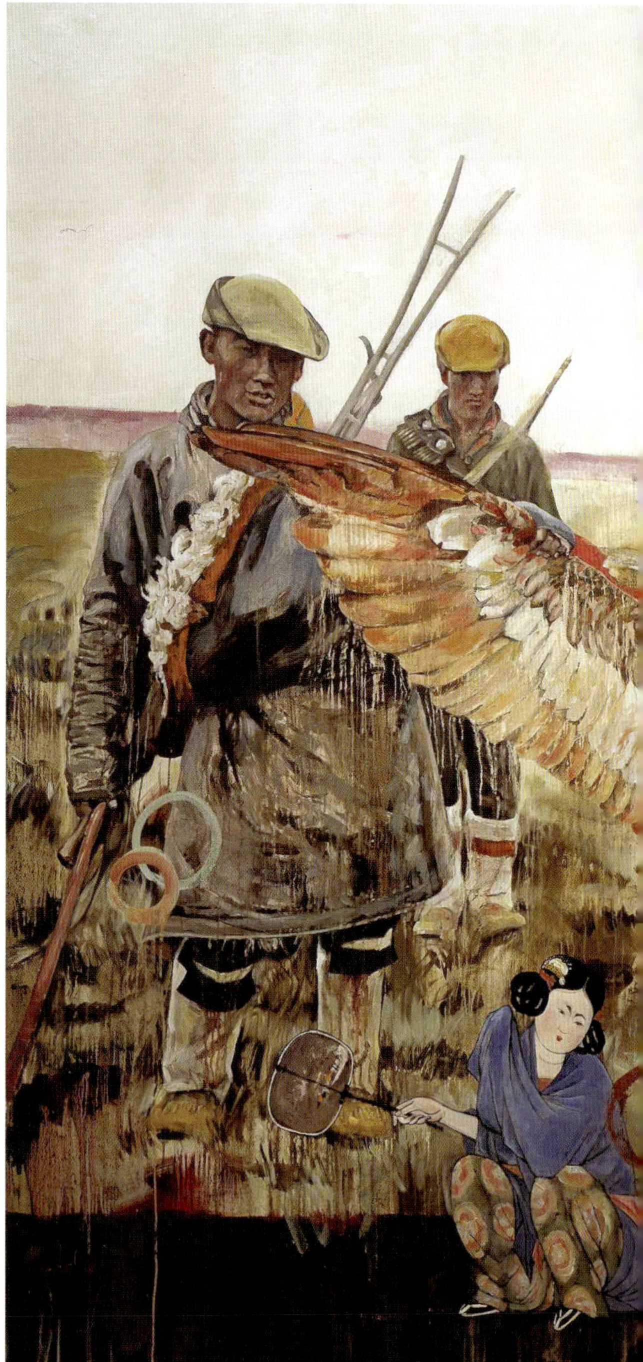

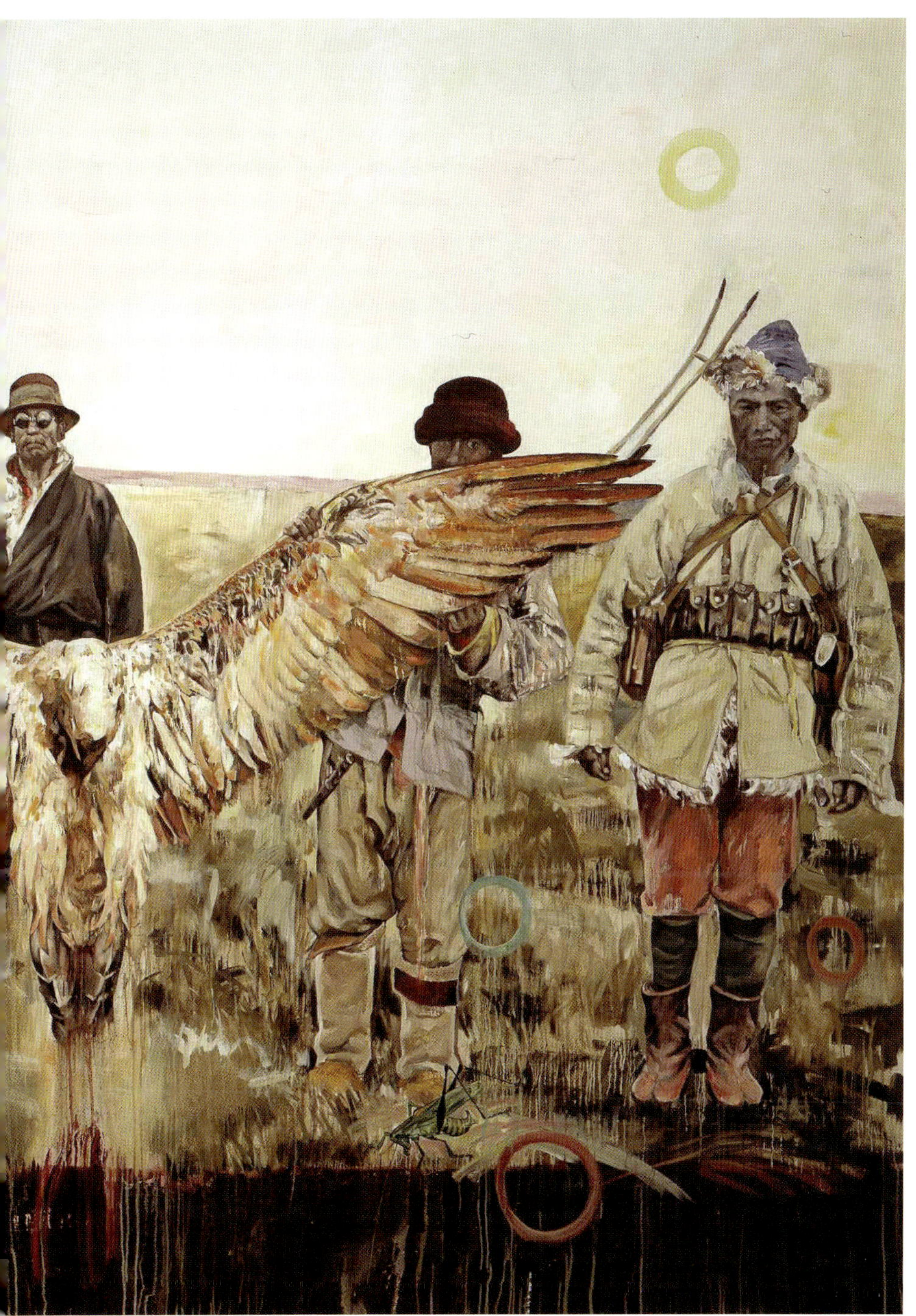

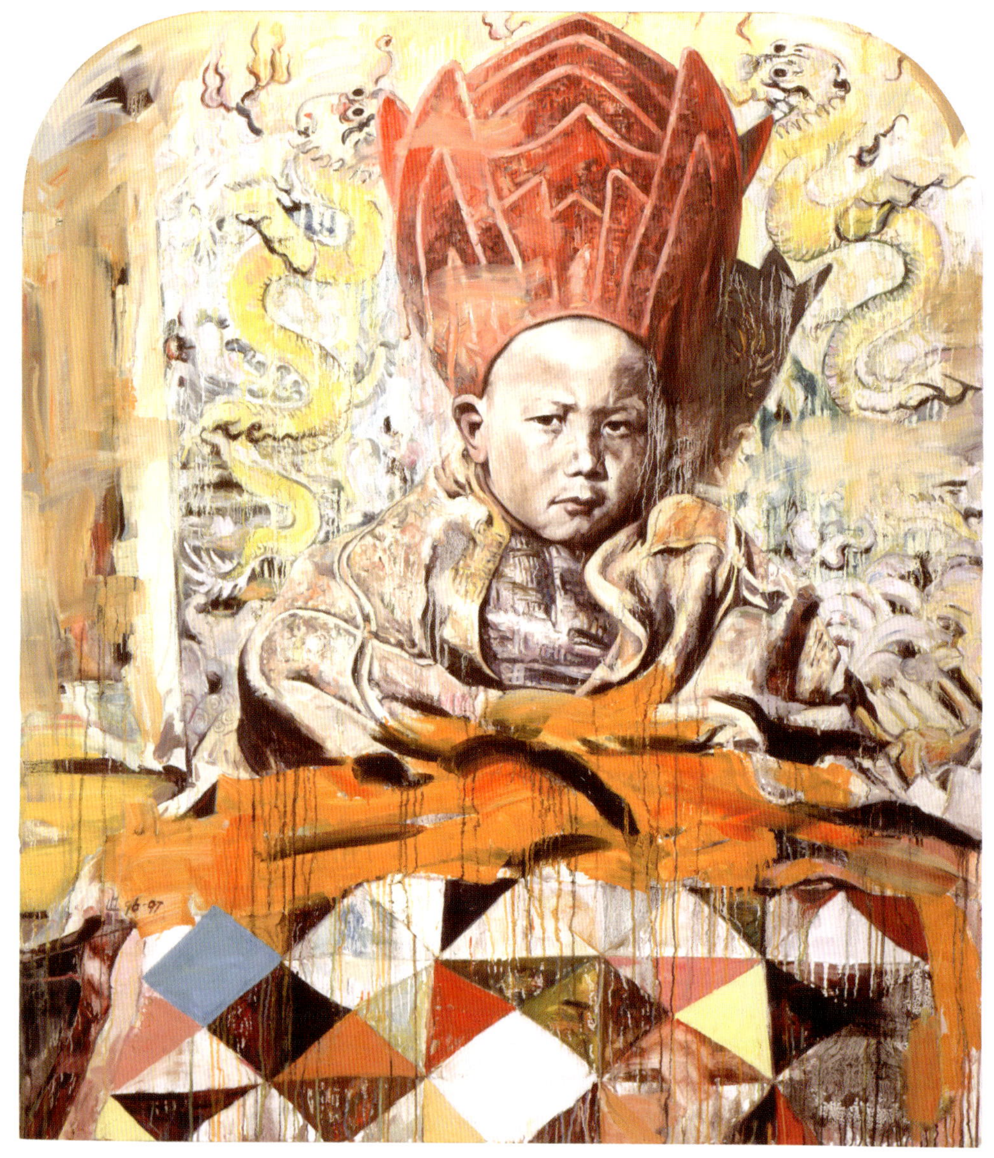

Baby Lama | 1997
oil on canvas | 68 x 60 inches | Private collection

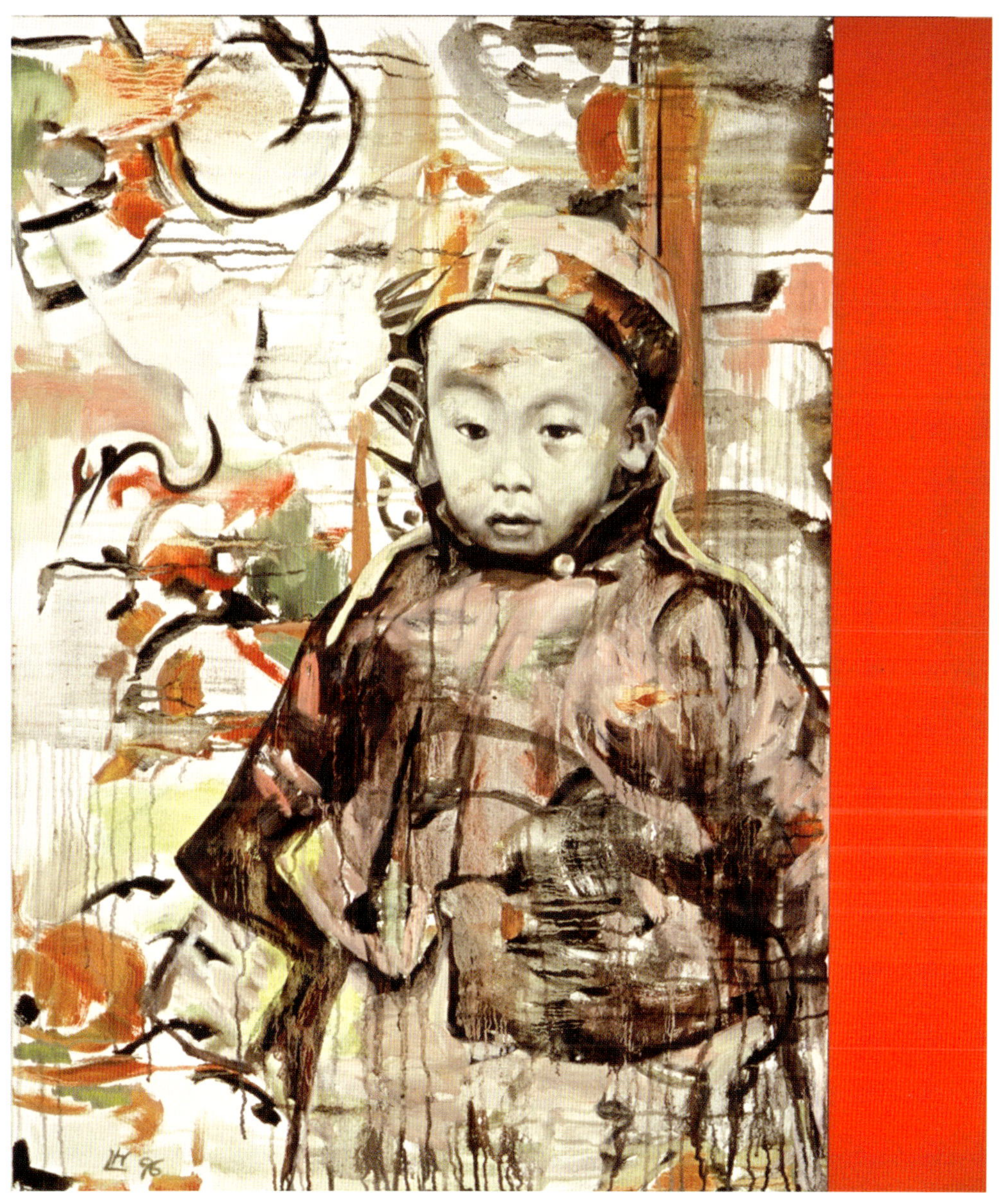

Cultural Relics 1: Pu Yi Three | 1996
oil on canvas, wood | 42 x 36 inches | Private collection

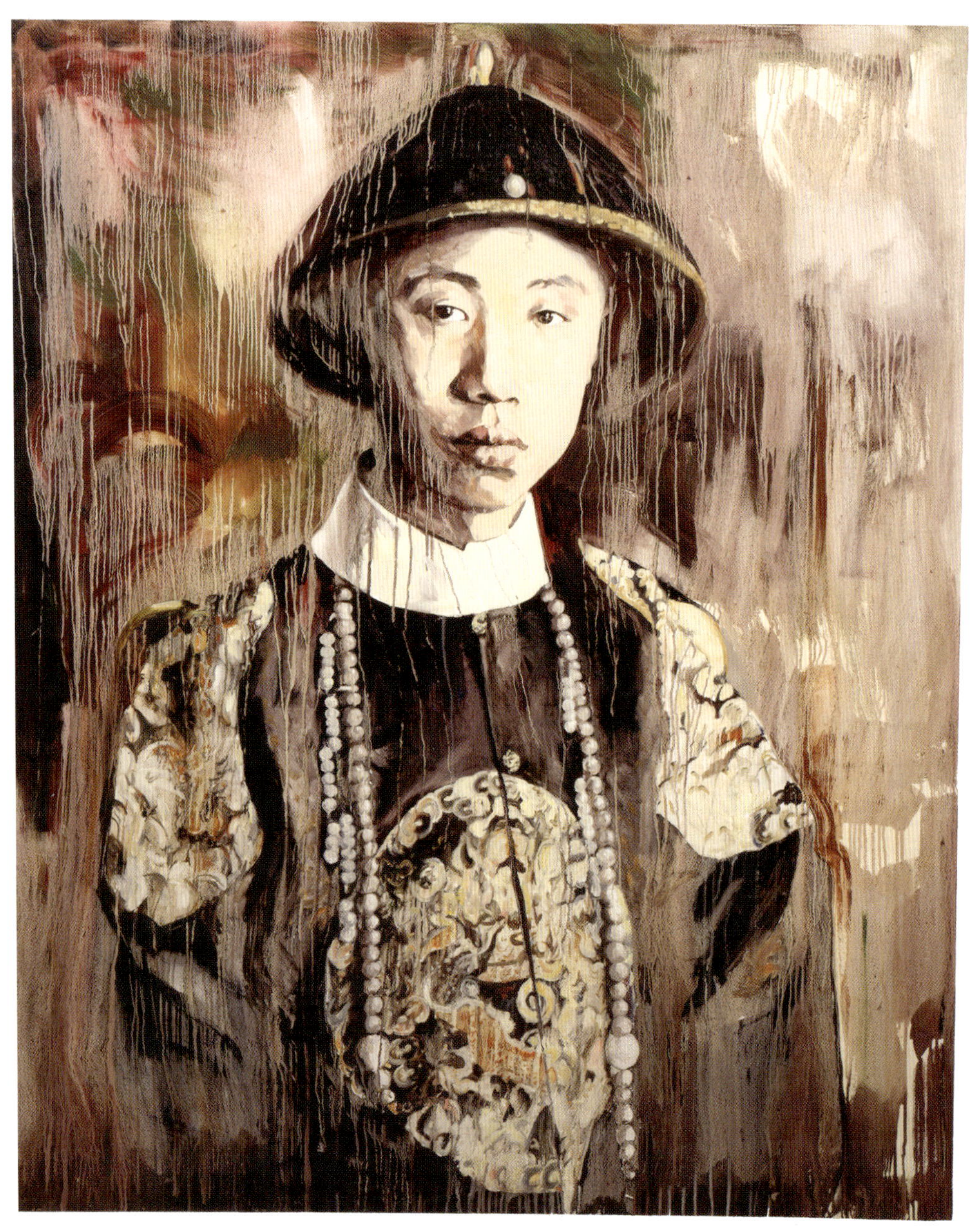

Baby King | 1995
oil on canvas | 72 x 60 inches | Private collection

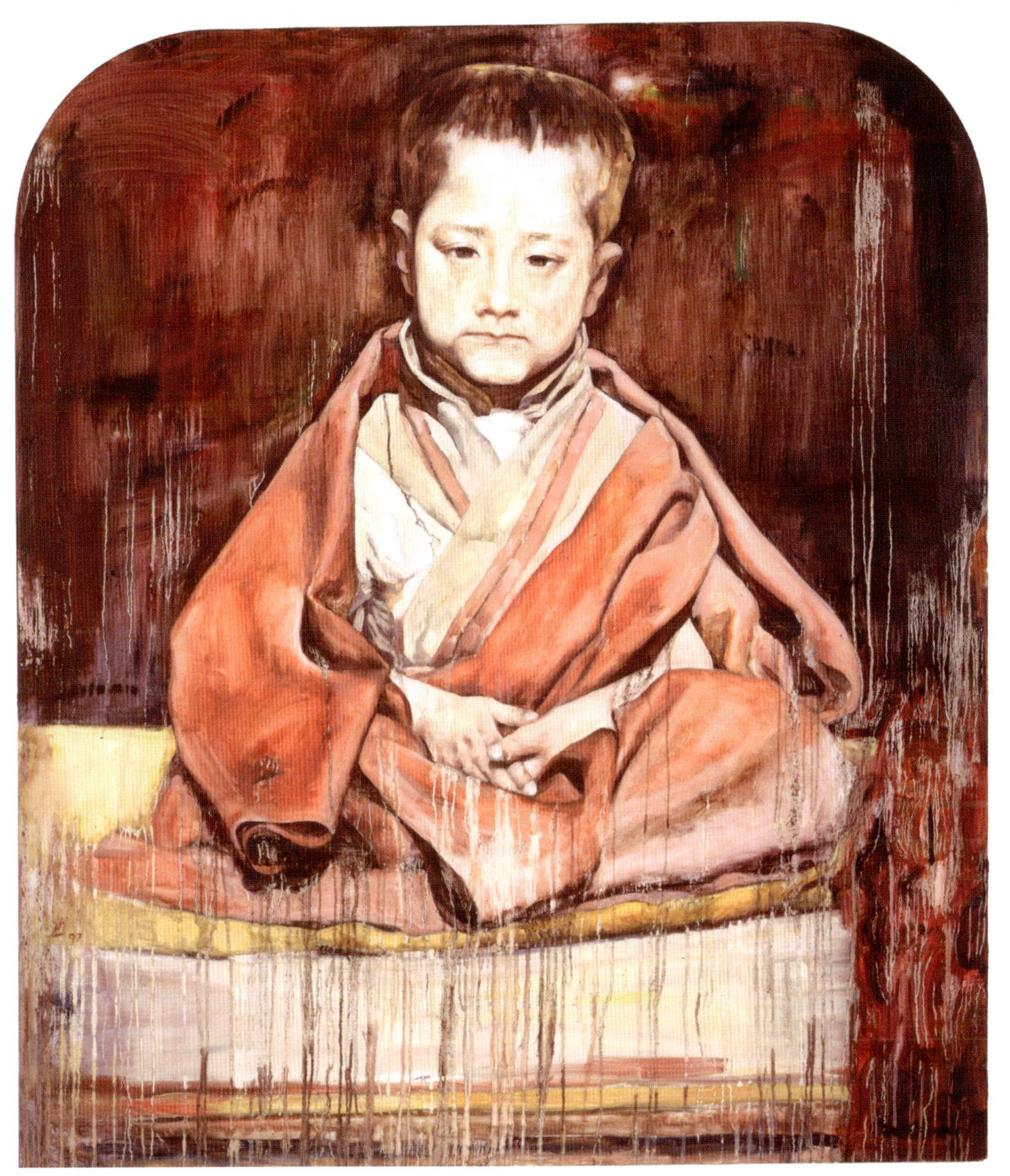

Enlightenment | 1997

oil on canvas | 68 x 60 inches | Private collection

Family | 1991
oil on canvas with painted
wooden boxes and a tea set
108 x 72 x 12 inches
Private collection

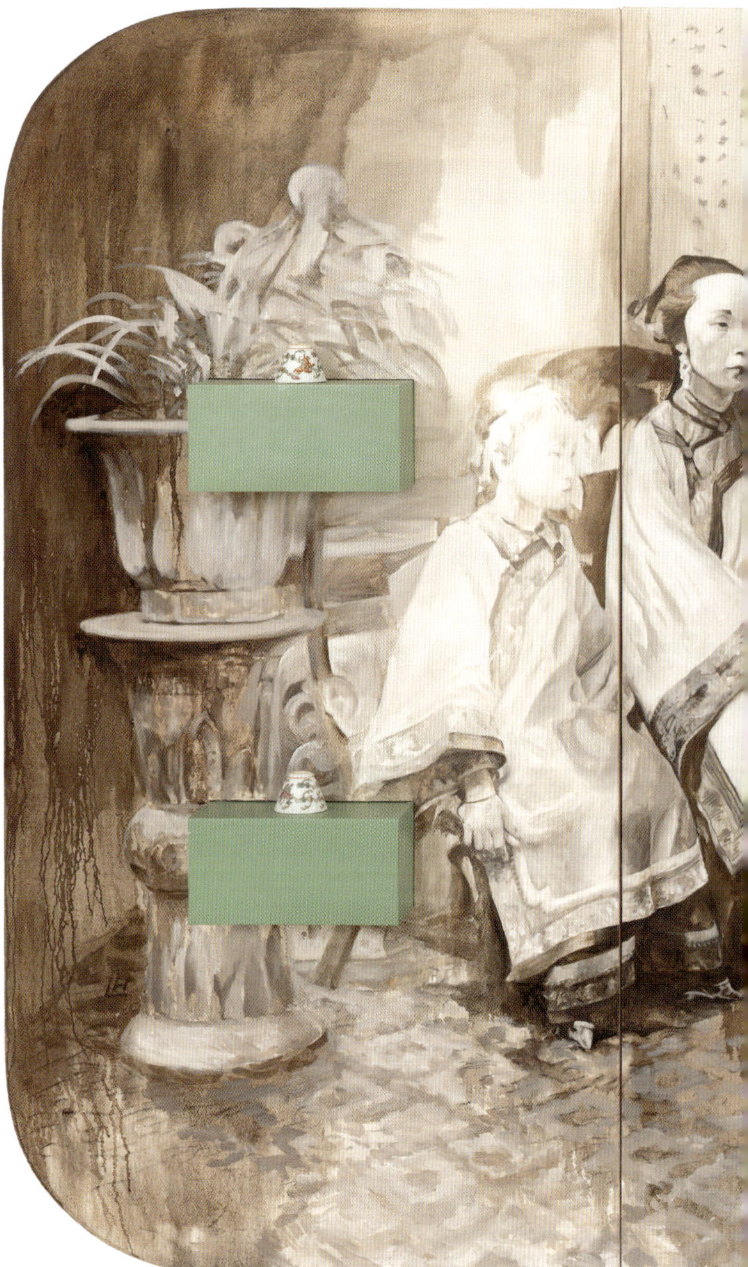

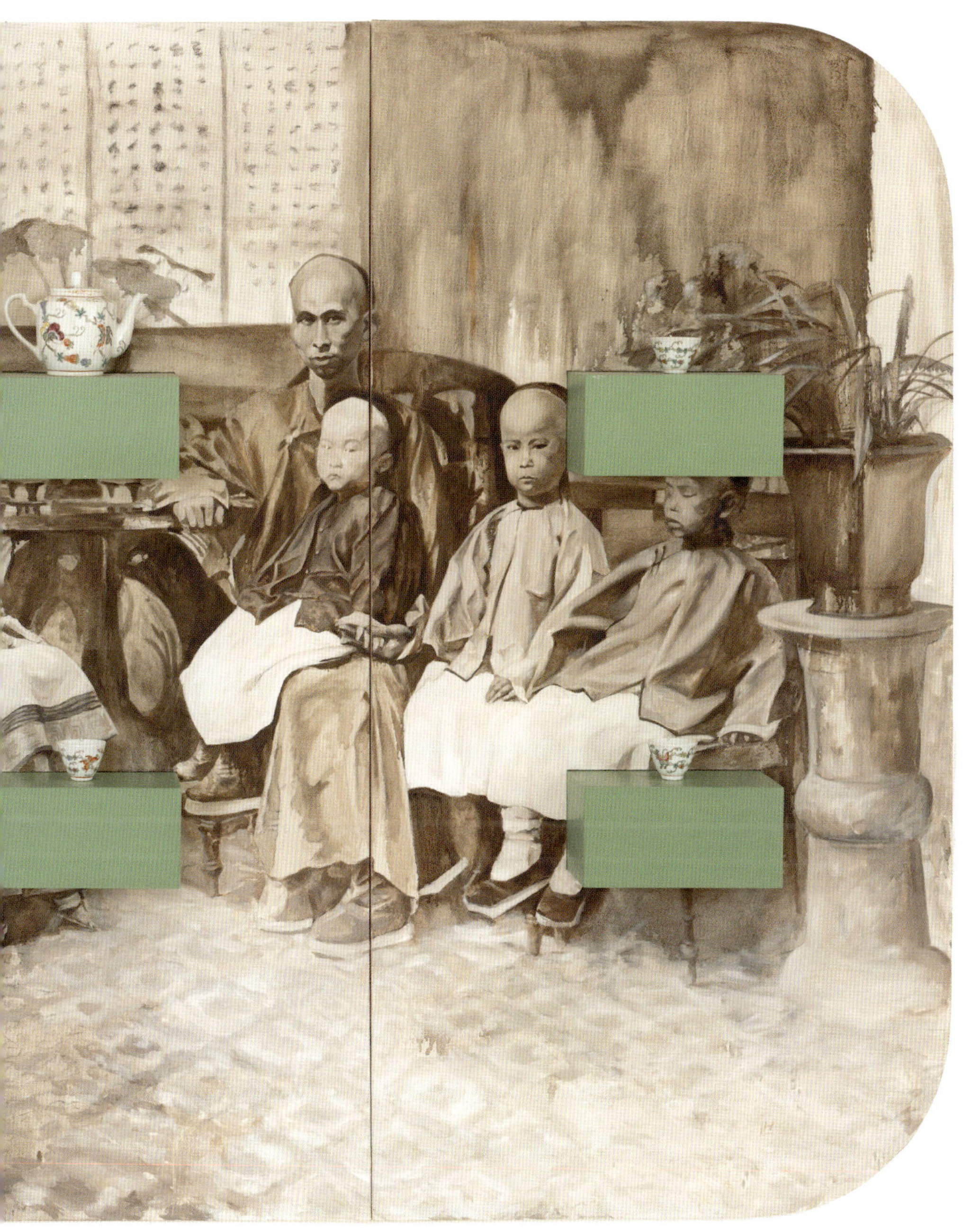

Chinese Profiles

The Chinese Profile paintings of 1998 were based on the anthropological photographs of John Thompson, a Scottish photographer who went to China during the 1860s. I decided to turn the Chinese "types" Thompson photographed in profile into a kind of refusal, a refusal to turn the head and return the gaze. So, I don't think of the women in the Chinese Profile paintings as anthropological subjects but rather as monuments etched in the grandeur of themselves. In my paintings, they are refusing to acknowledge the power of the camera.

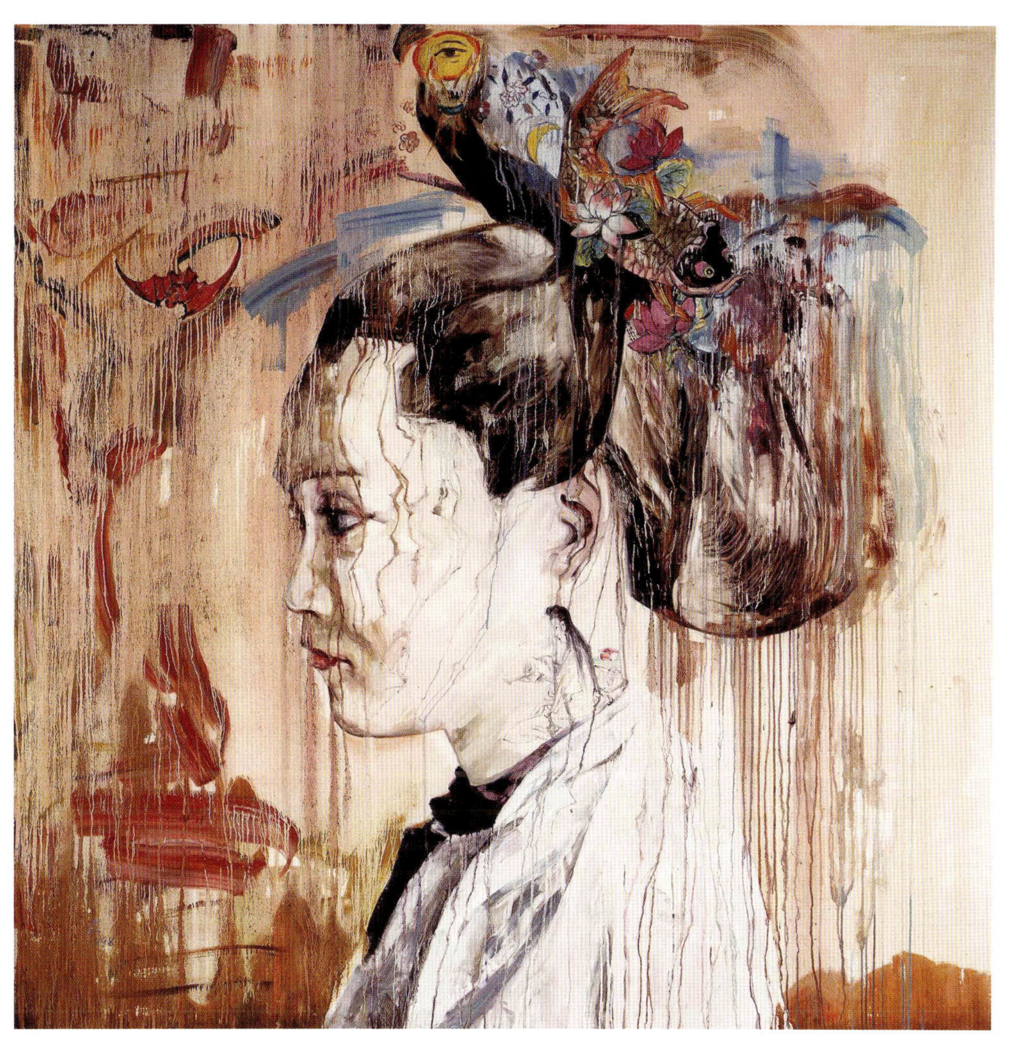

Chinese Profile IV | 1998
oil on canvas | 80 x 80 inches | Collection of the artist

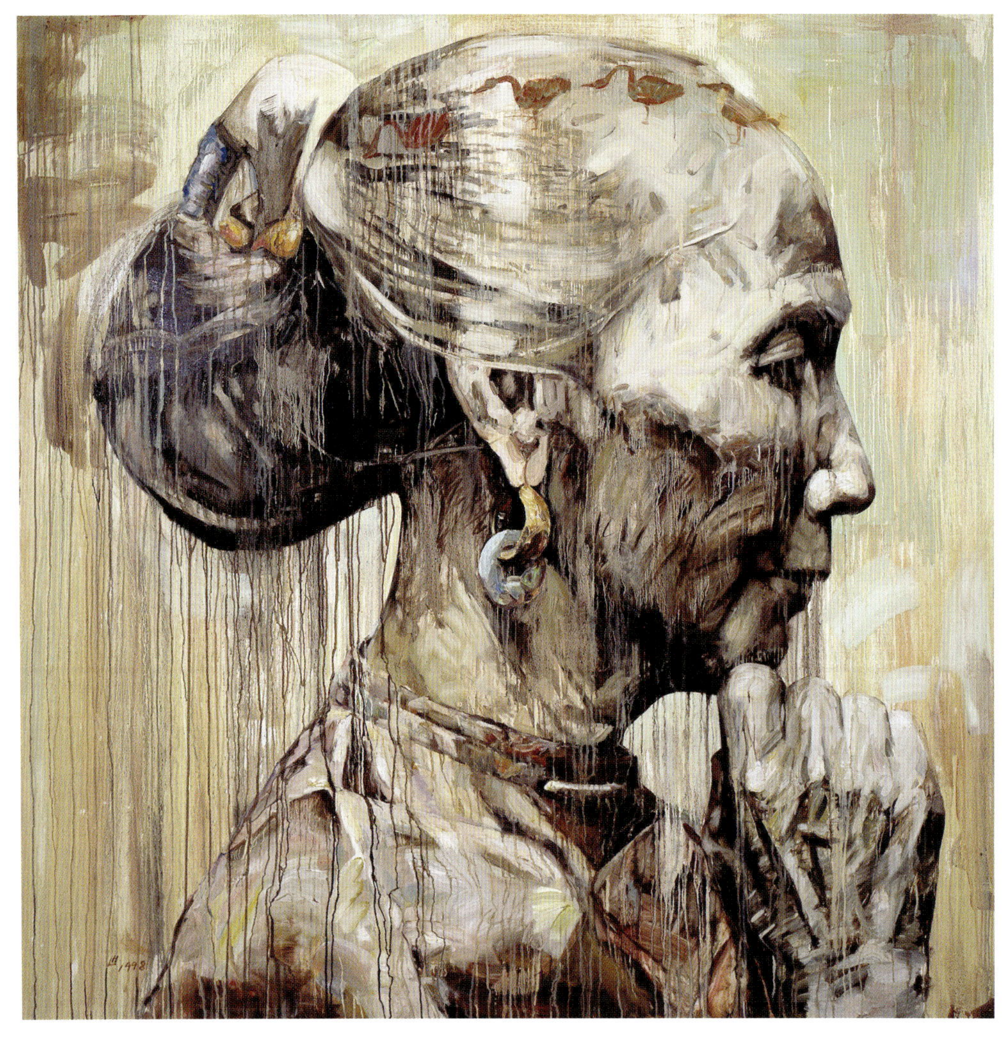

Chinese Profile III | 1998
mixed media with resin | 80 x 80 inches | Private collection

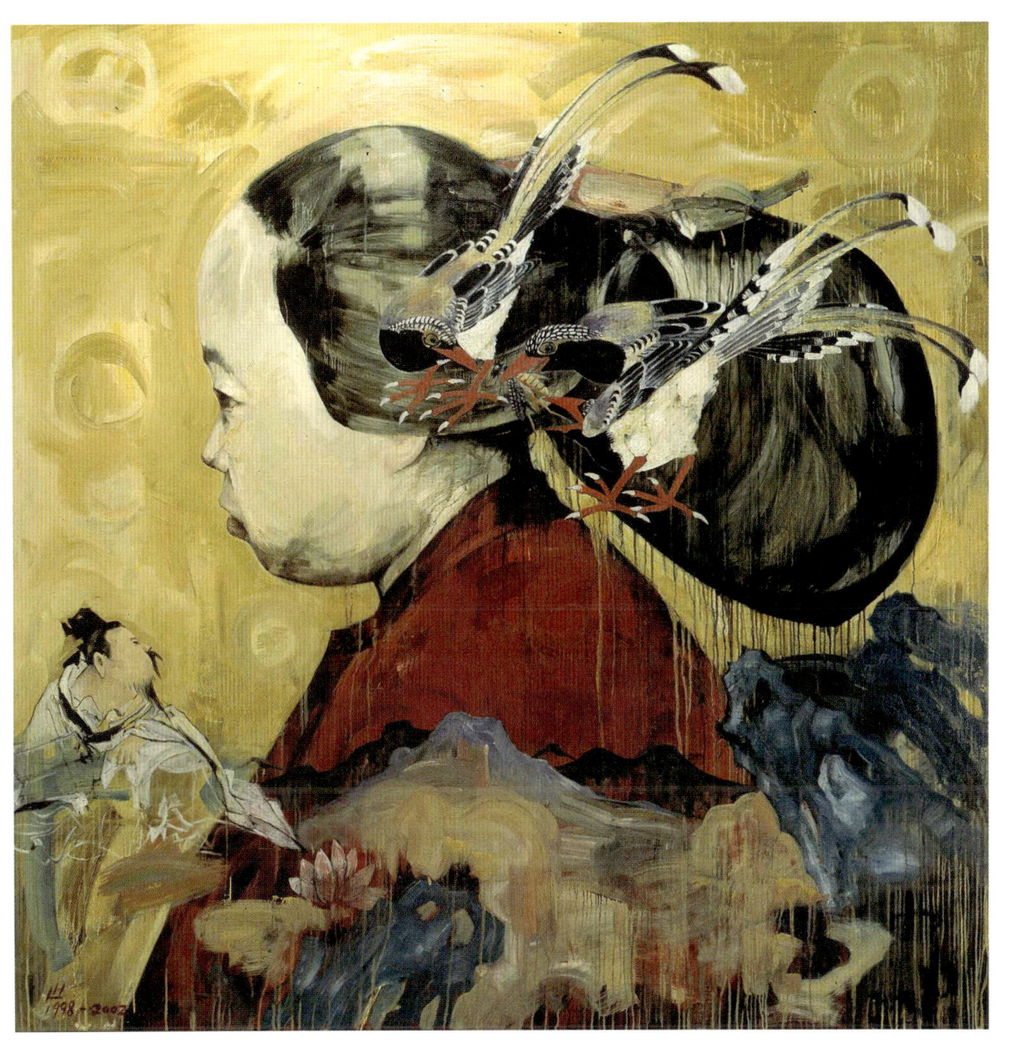

Chinese Profile I | 1998

oil on canvas | 80 x 80 inches | Private collection

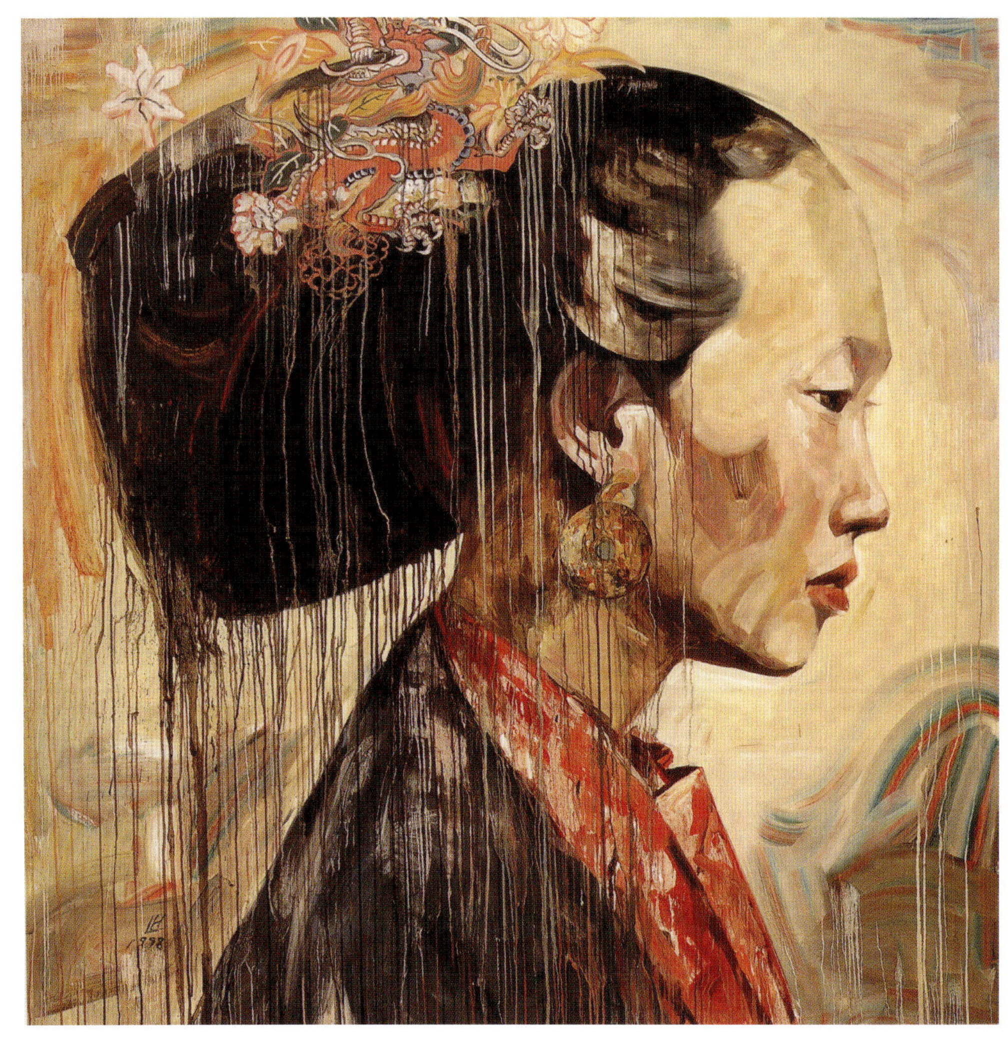

Chinese Profile II | 1998
oil on canvas | 80 x 80 inches | San José Museum of Art

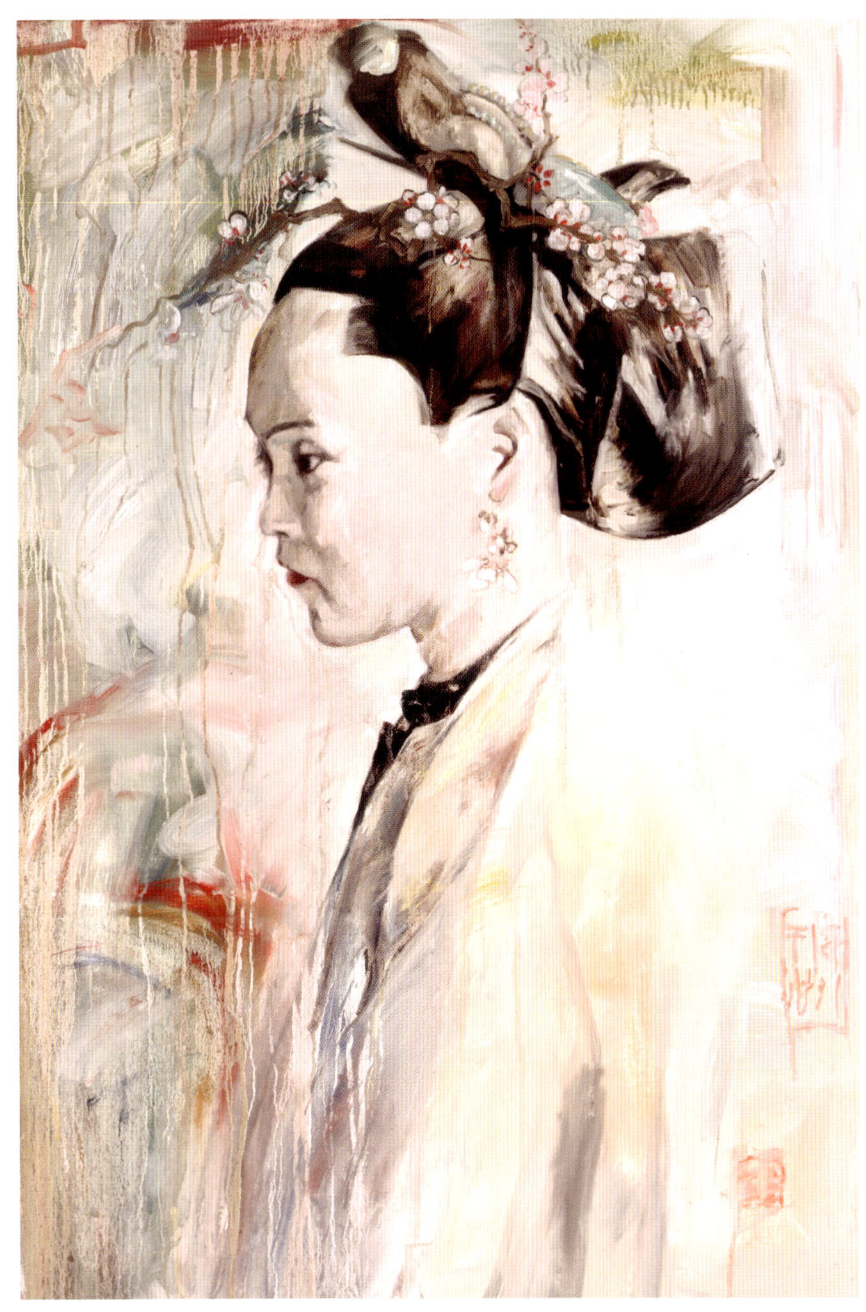

Chinese Type III | 1998
oil on canvas | 48 x 32 inches | Private collection

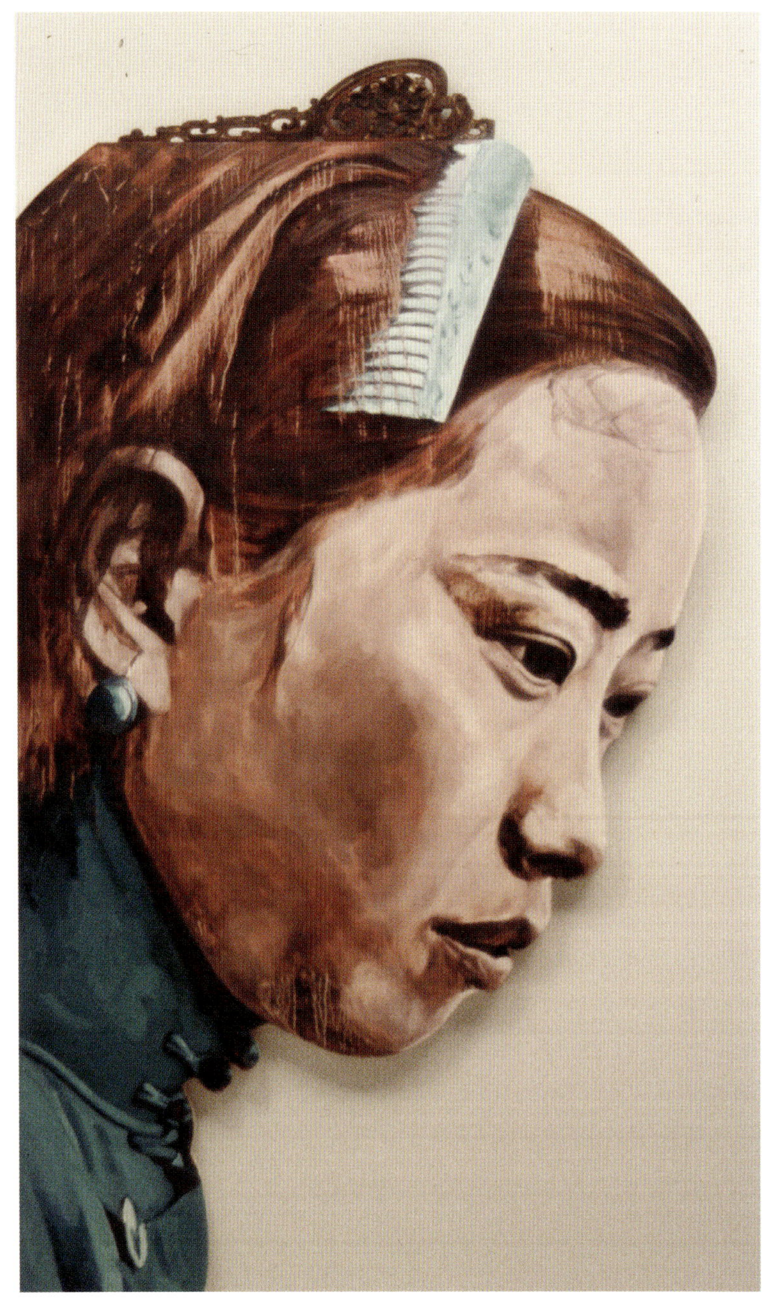

Daughter-in-Law | 1993
oil on canvas, antique architectural wall panel | 69.5 x 40 inches | Private collection

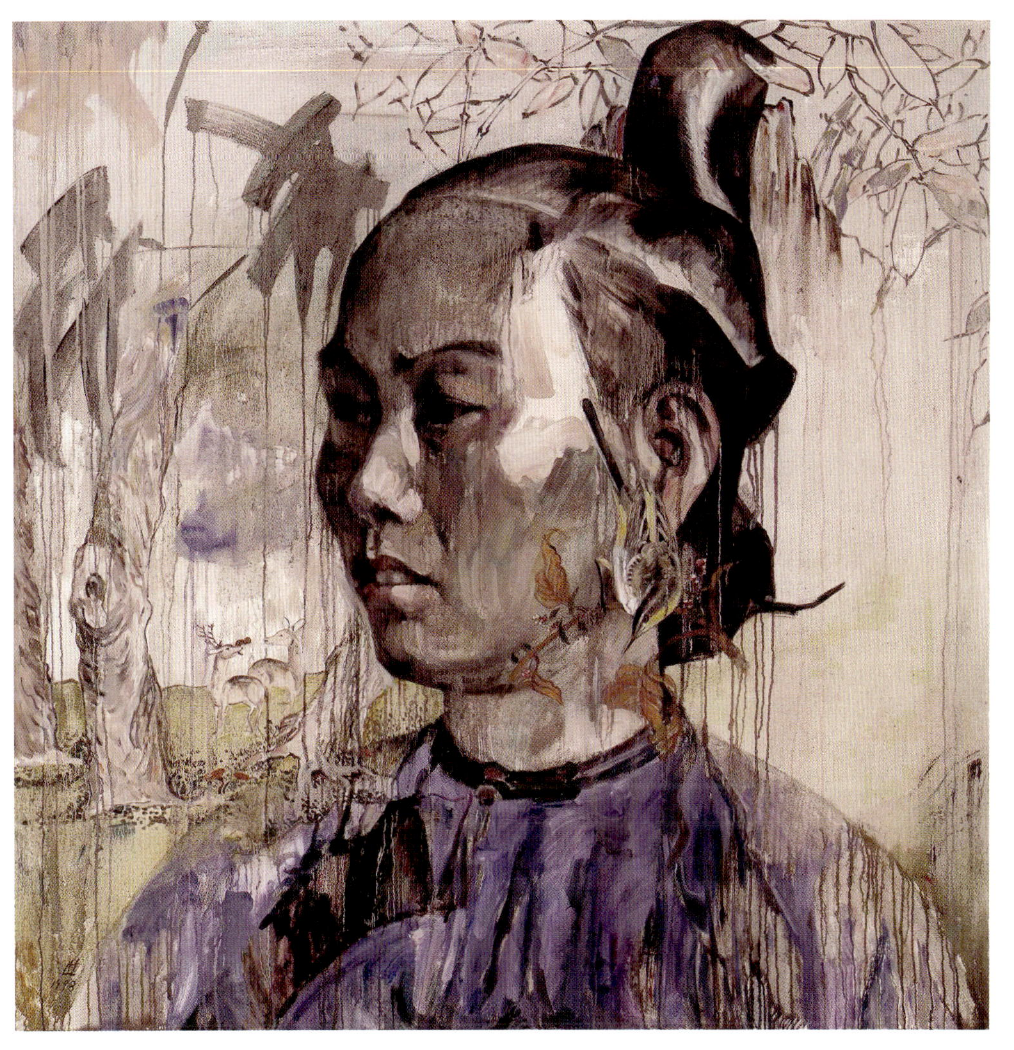

Blue Blouse | 1998

oil on canvas | 66 x 66 inches | Private collection

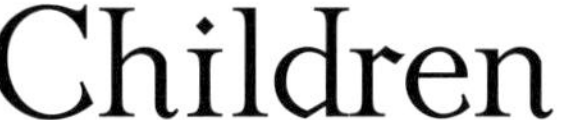

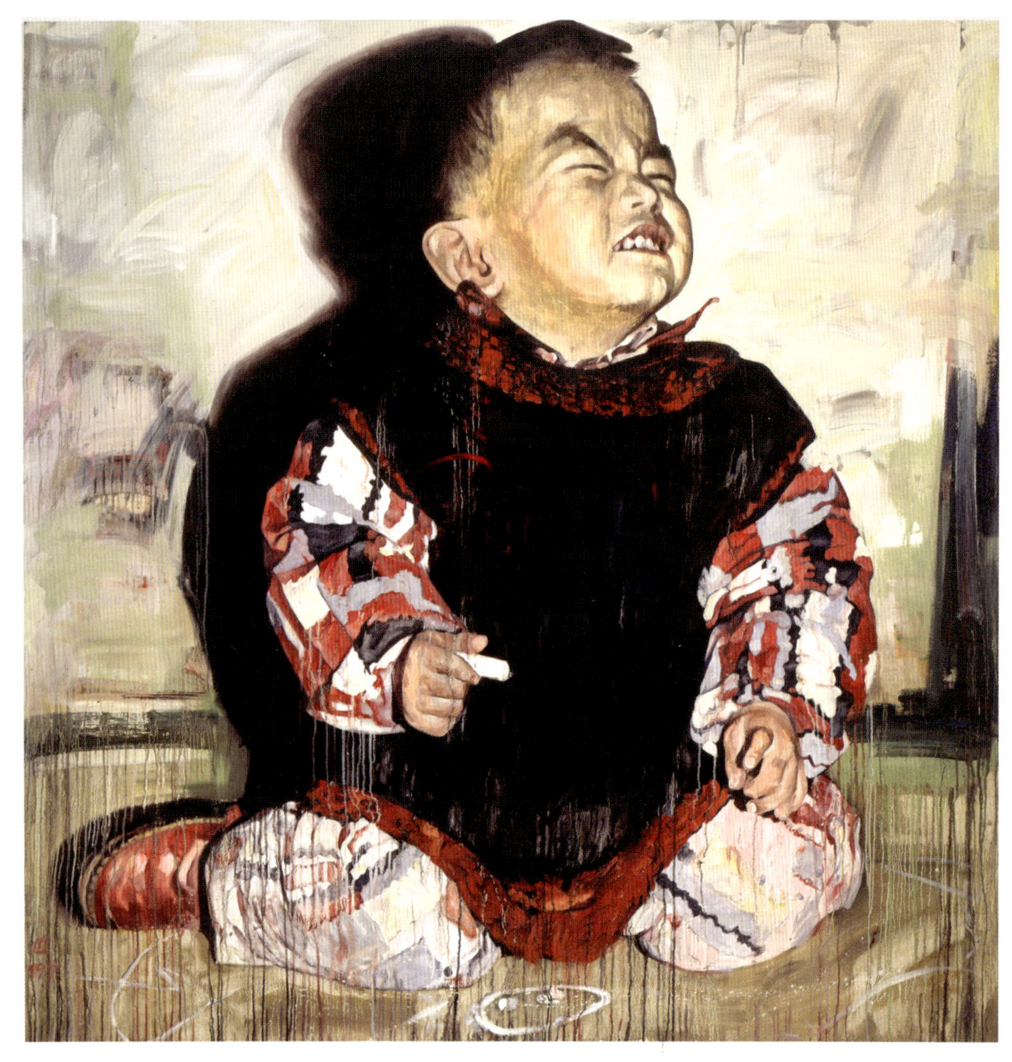

Little Artist | 1998
oil on canvas | 80 x 80 inches | Private collection

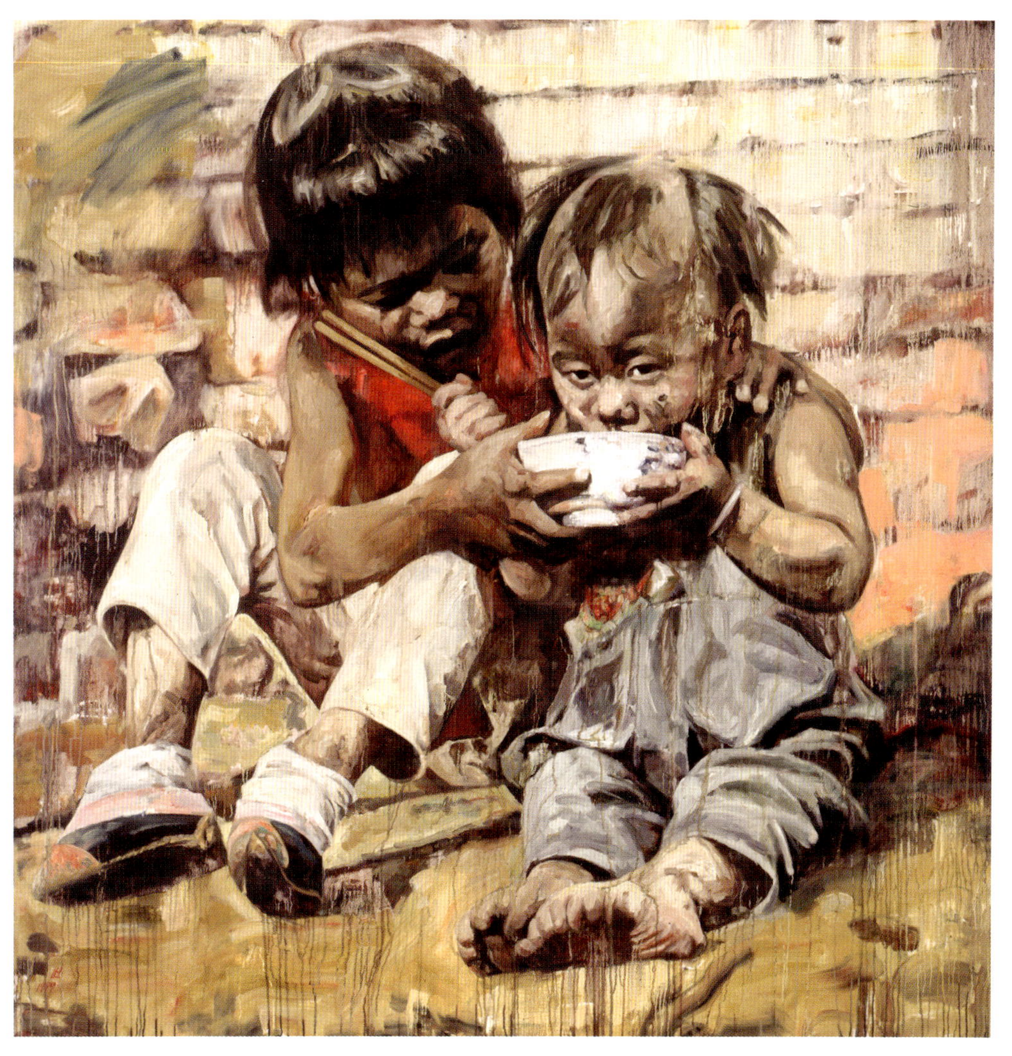

White Rice Bowl | 1997

oil on canvas | 80 x 80 inches | Private collection

In historical photographs children's images are fixed in a chemical surface and yet the children in old photographs are forever young. Today some would be eighty or one hundred years old— most are gone. Thus, the children in my paintings, while forever young, are also as old as ancestors. They are photo-chemical ghosts.

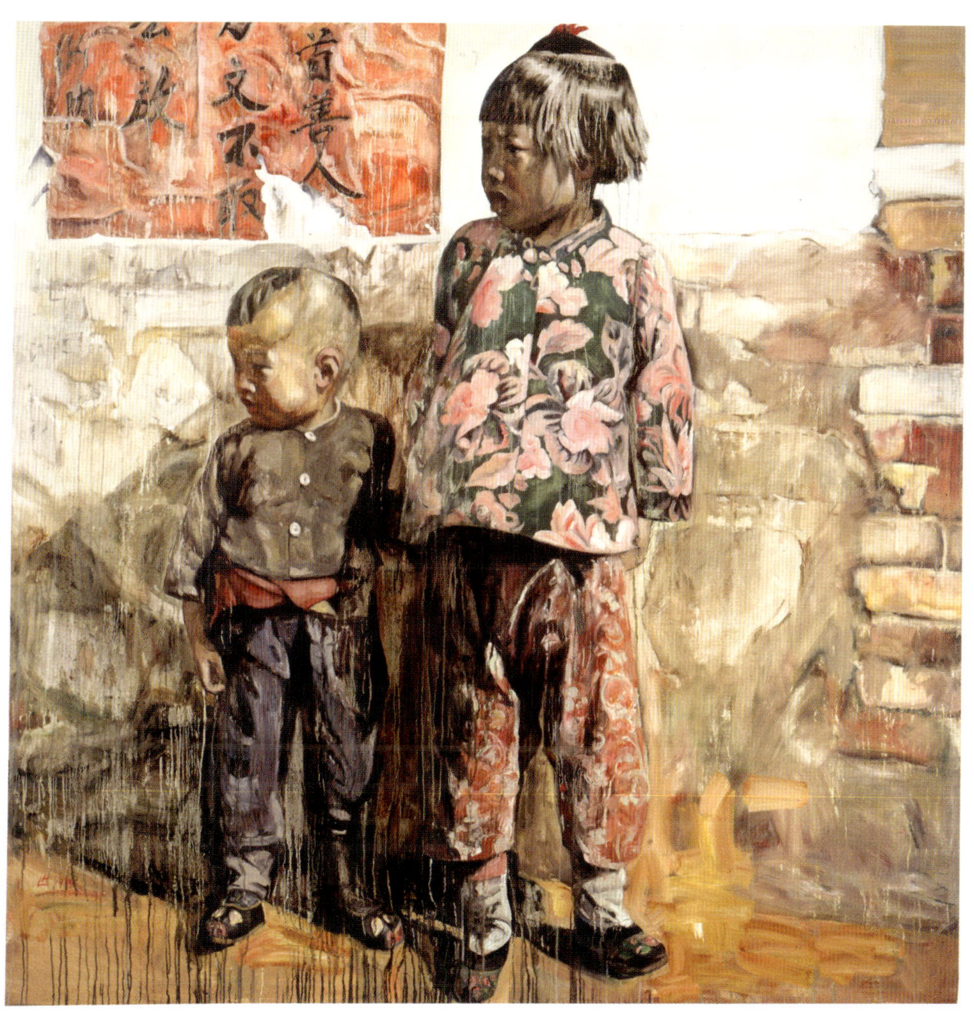

Red Wall Poster (Execution) | 1997

oil on canvas | 80 x 80 inches | Private collection

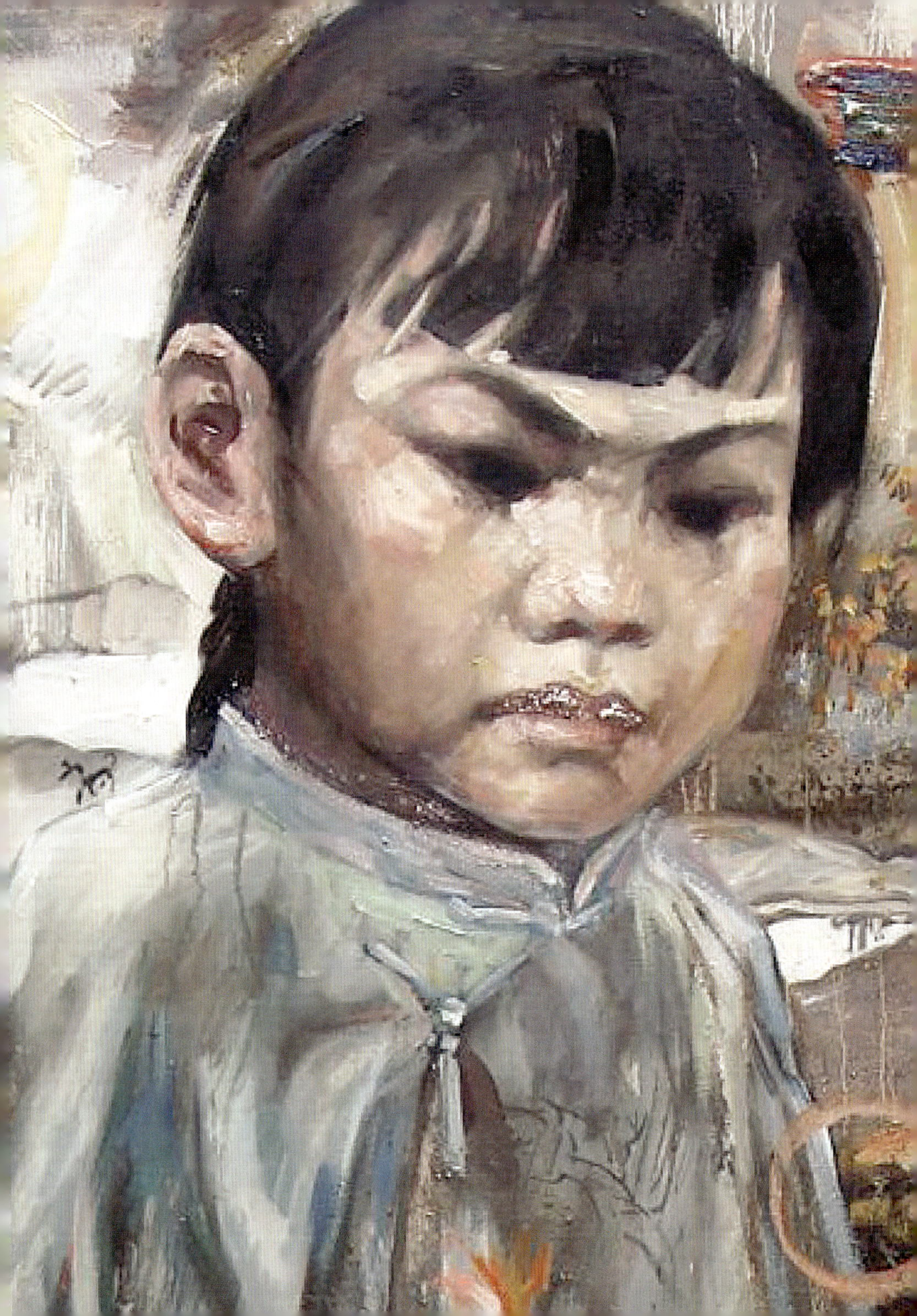

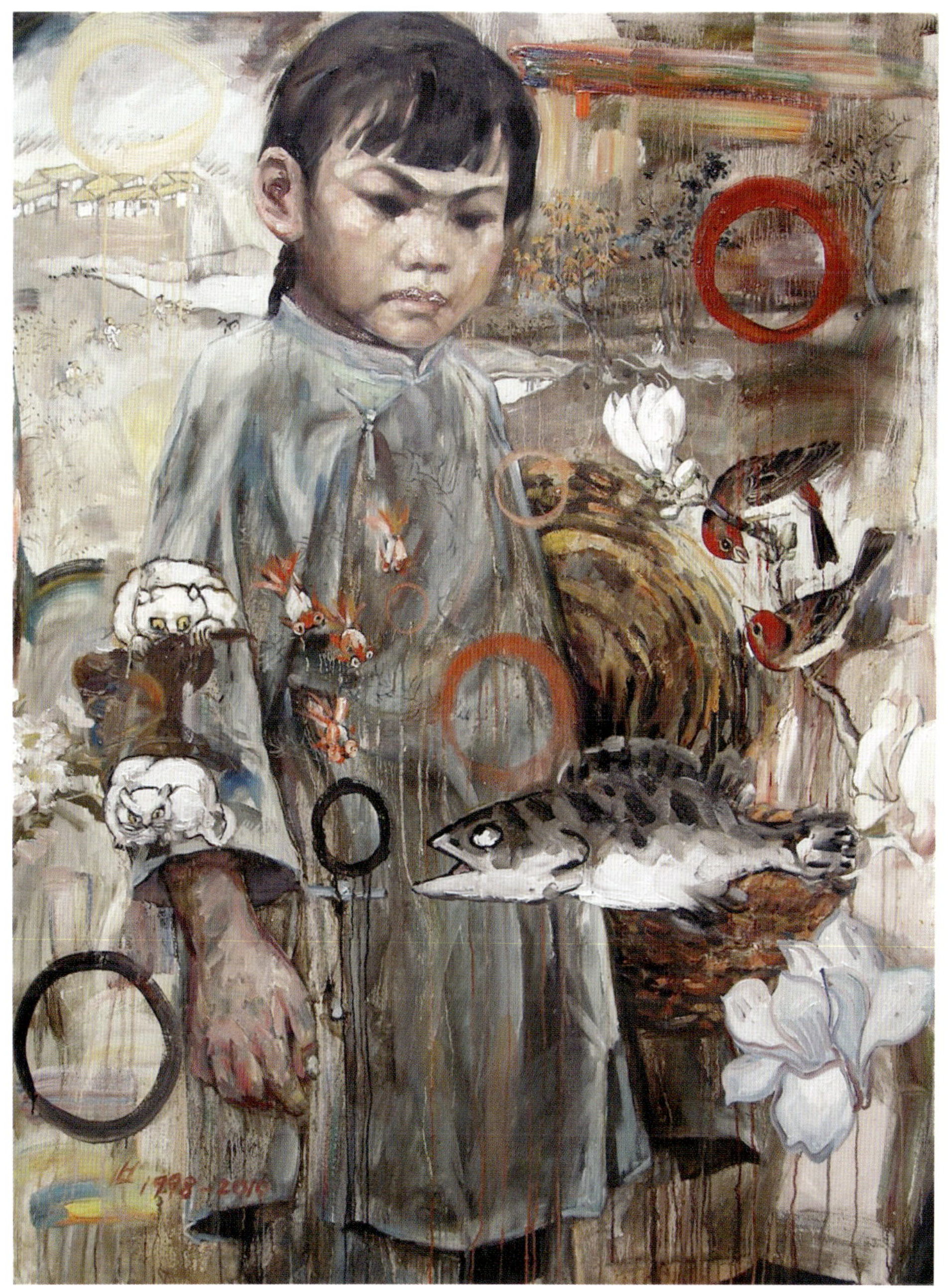

Bystander | 1997
oil on canvas | 64 x 48 inches | Private collection

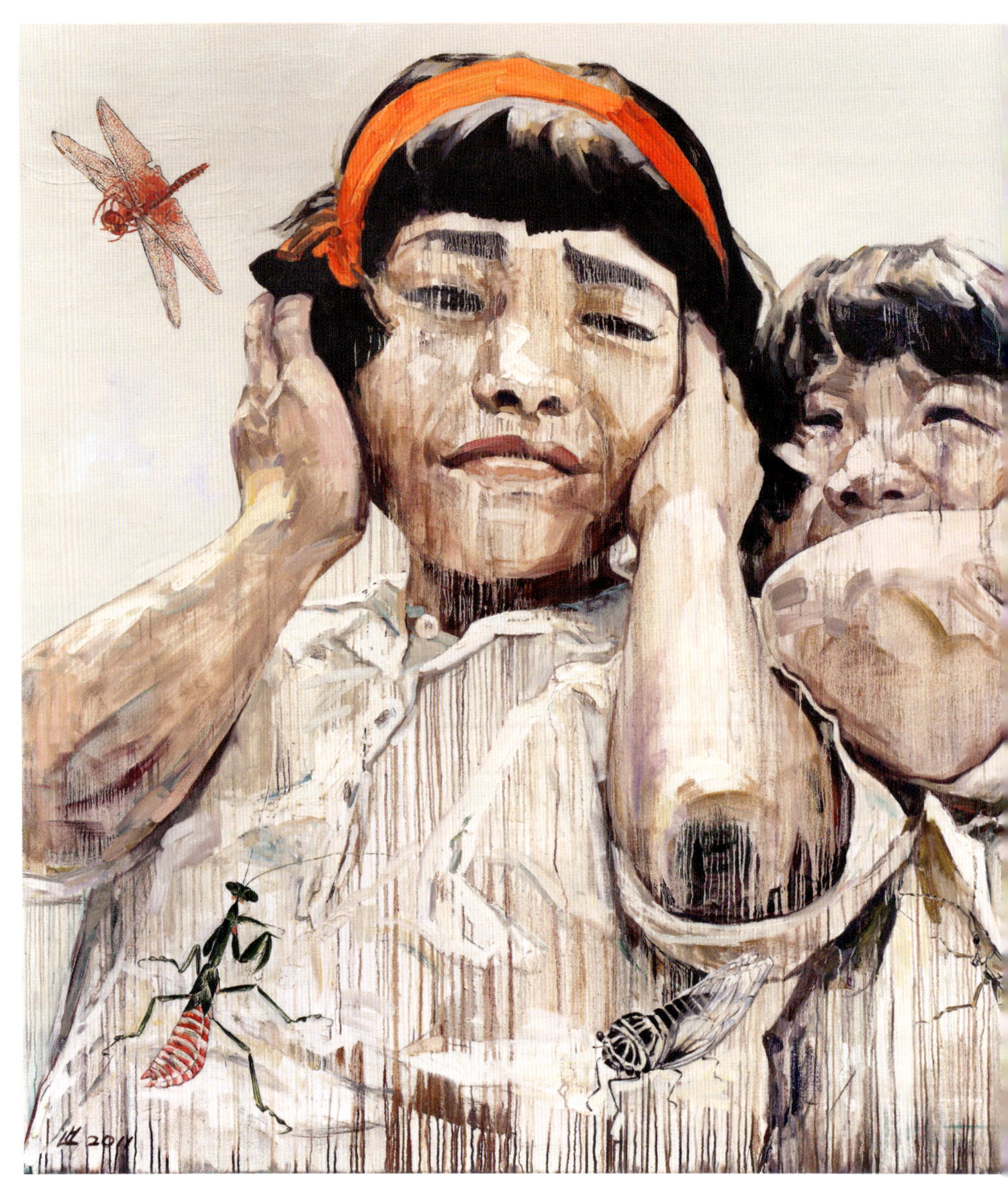

Jingzhe: First Spring Thunder | 2011
oil on canvas | 80 x 140 inches | Private collection

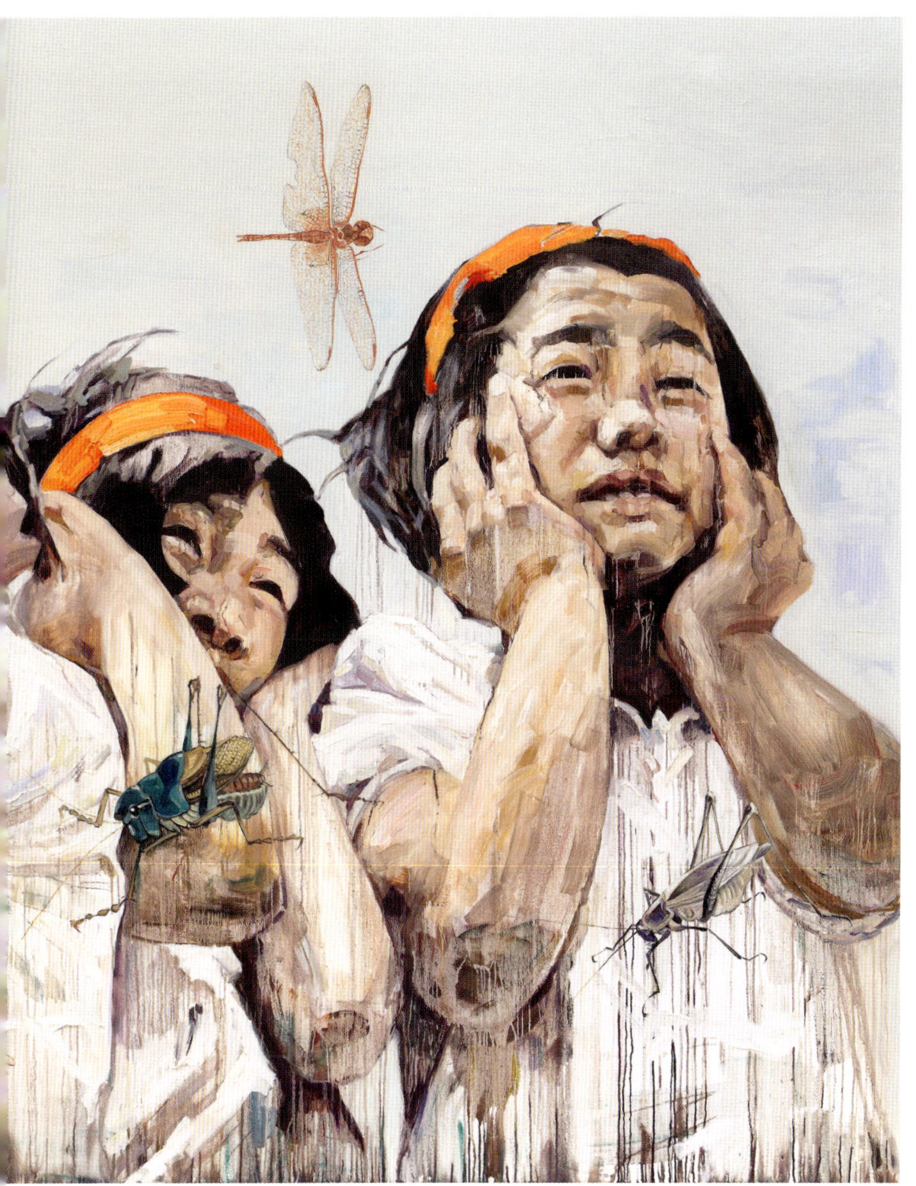

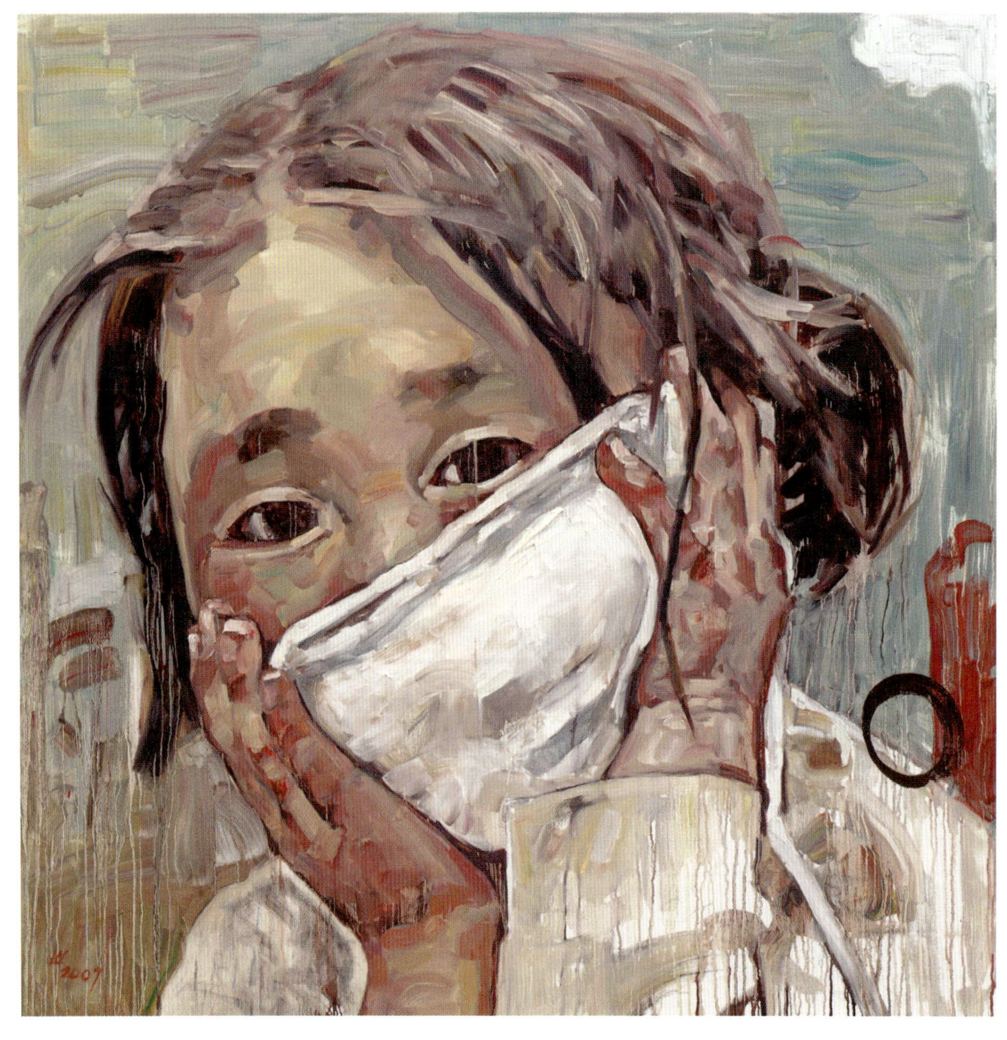

Apsaras Black | 2009
oil on canvas | 72 x 72 inches | Collection of the artist

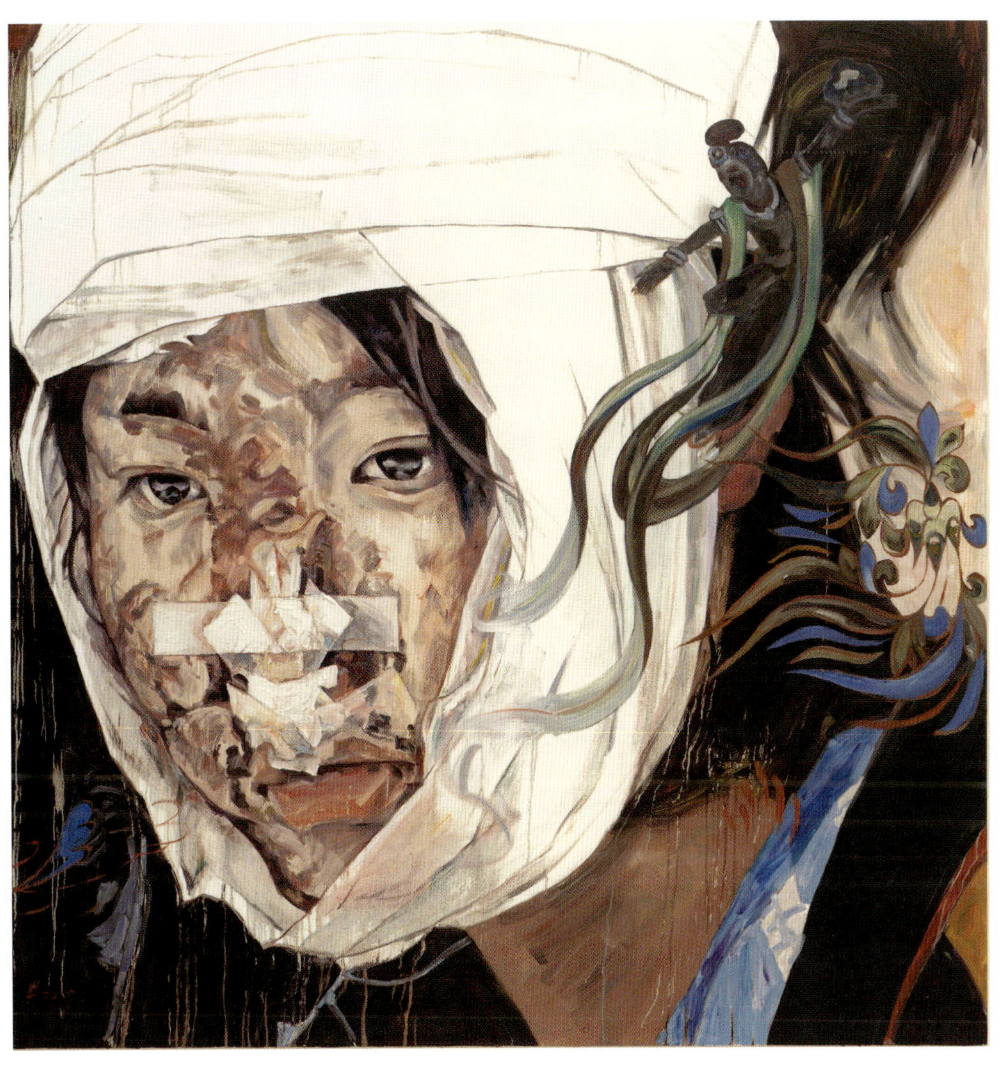

Apsaras Blue | 2009
oil on canvas | 72 x 72 inches | Collection of the artist

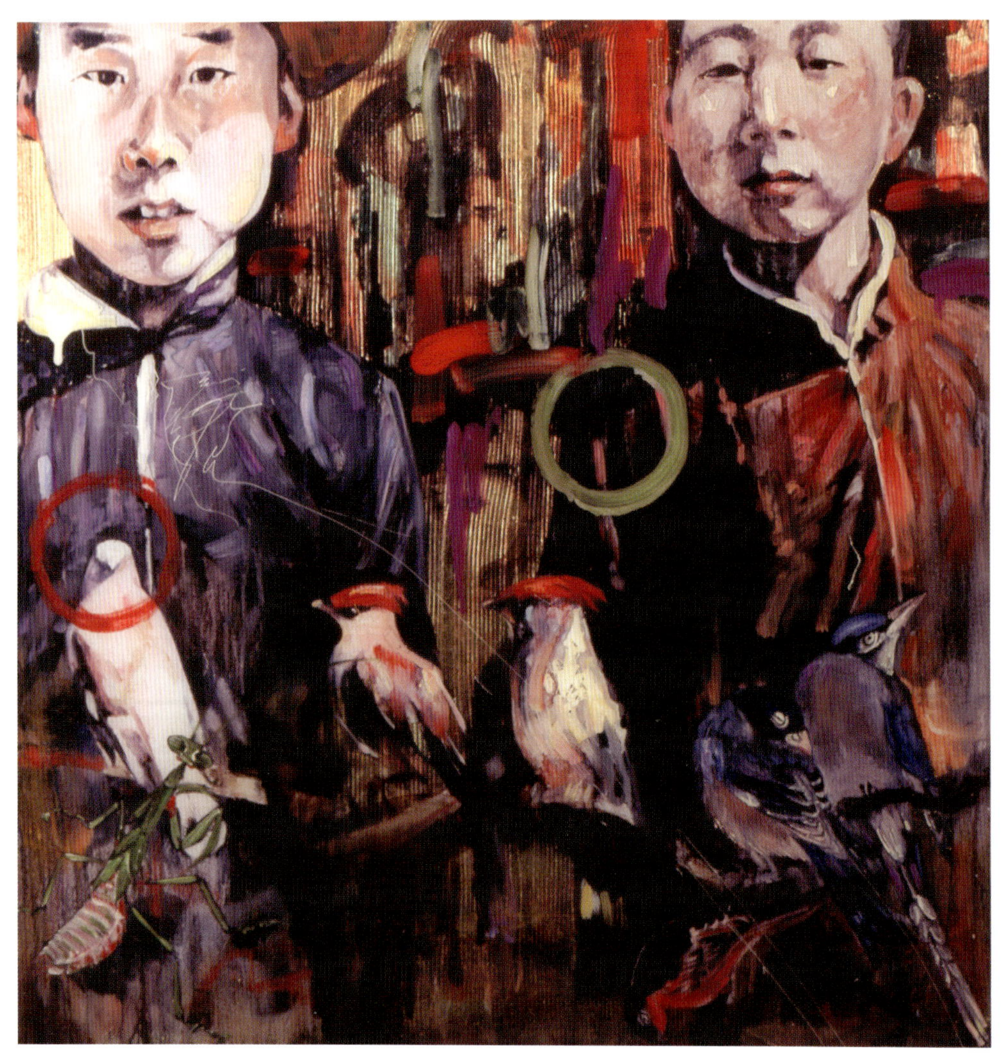

Boys and the Birds | 1998
oil on canvas | 36 x 36 inches | Private collection

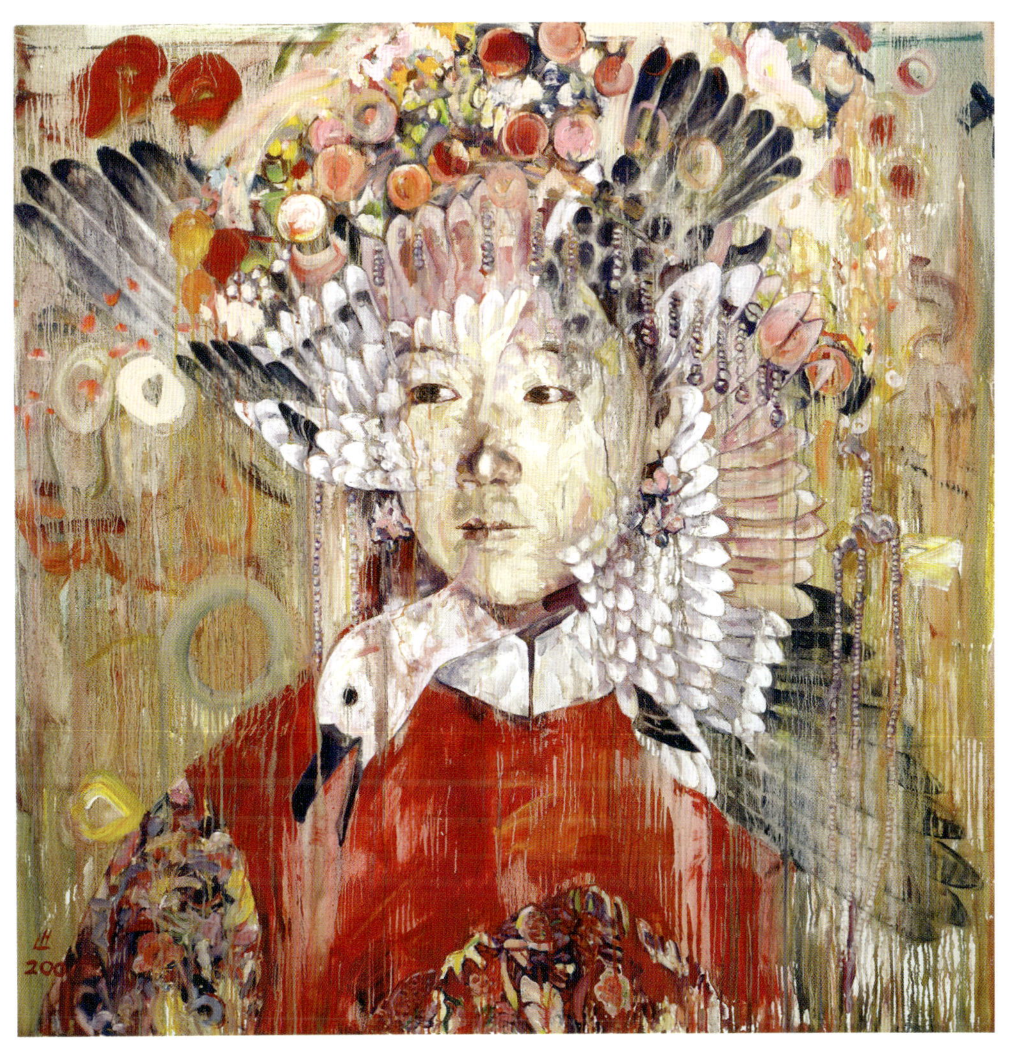

September | 2001
oil on canvas | 66 x 66 inches | Private collection

Band of Brothers

2011 | oil on canvas

80 x 120 inches

Private collection

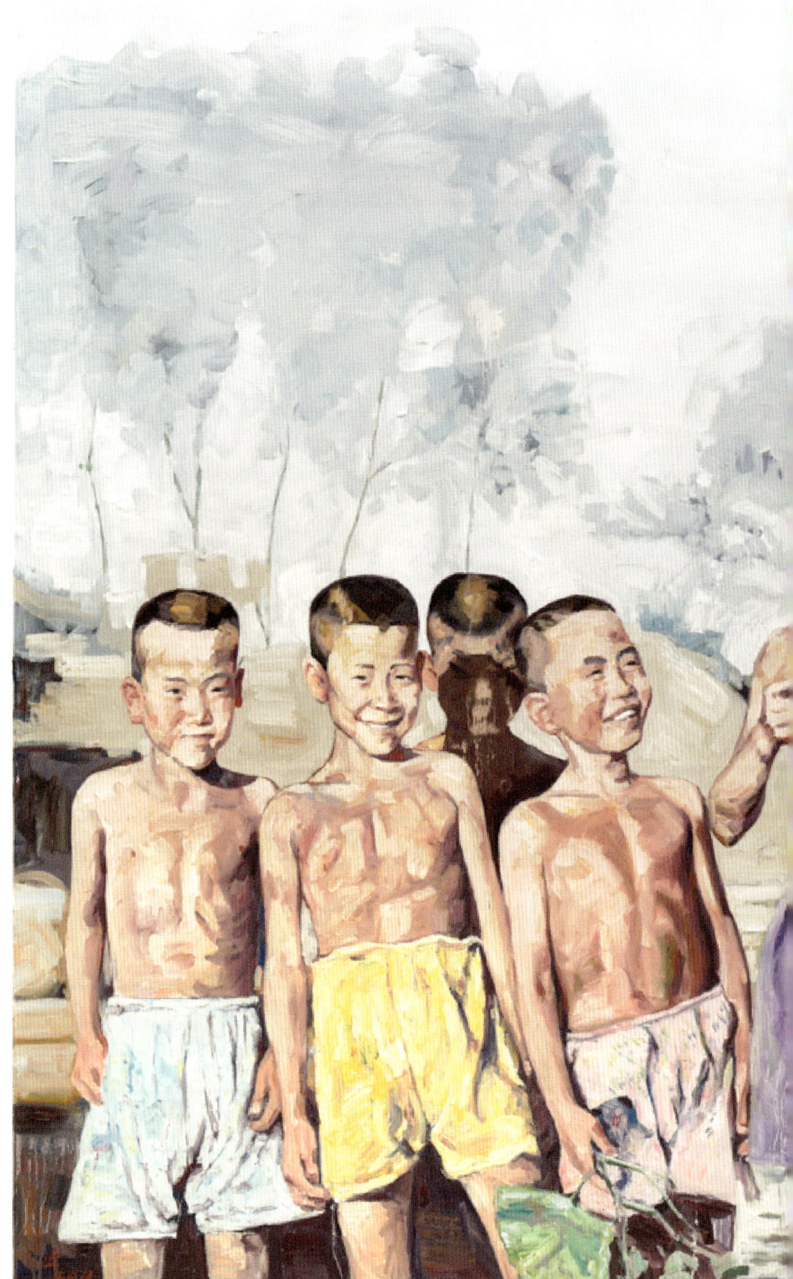

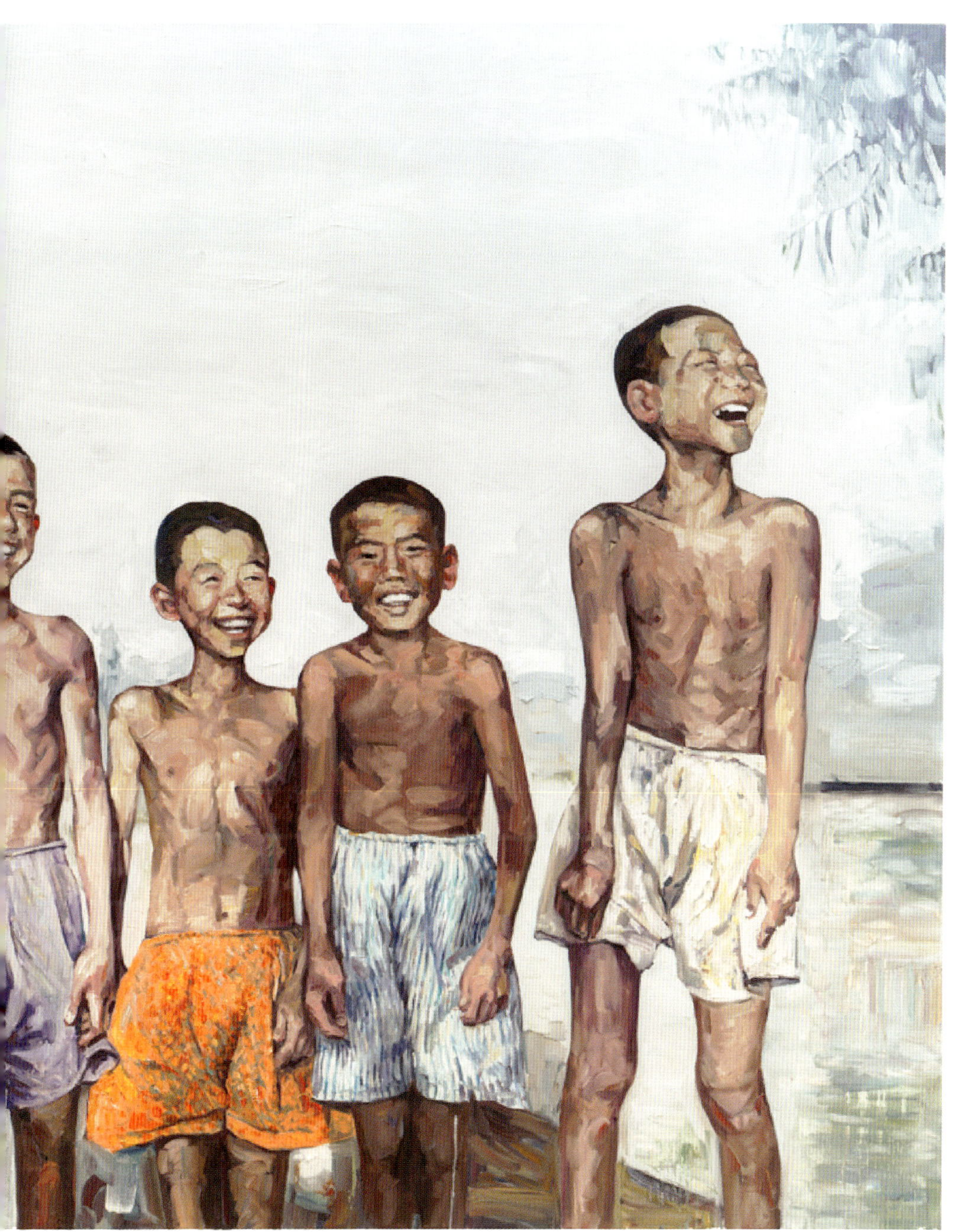

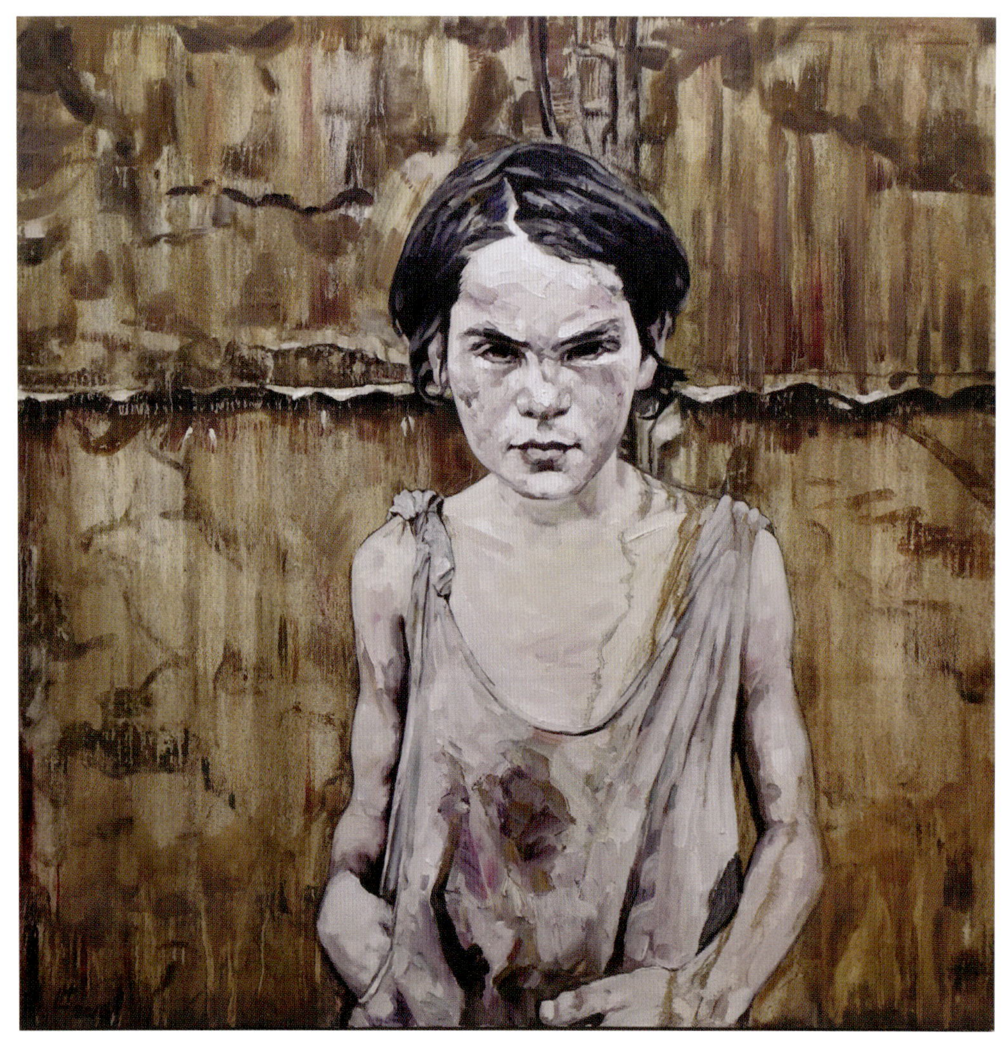

Damaged Child | 2015

oil on canvas | 48 x 48 inches | Private collection

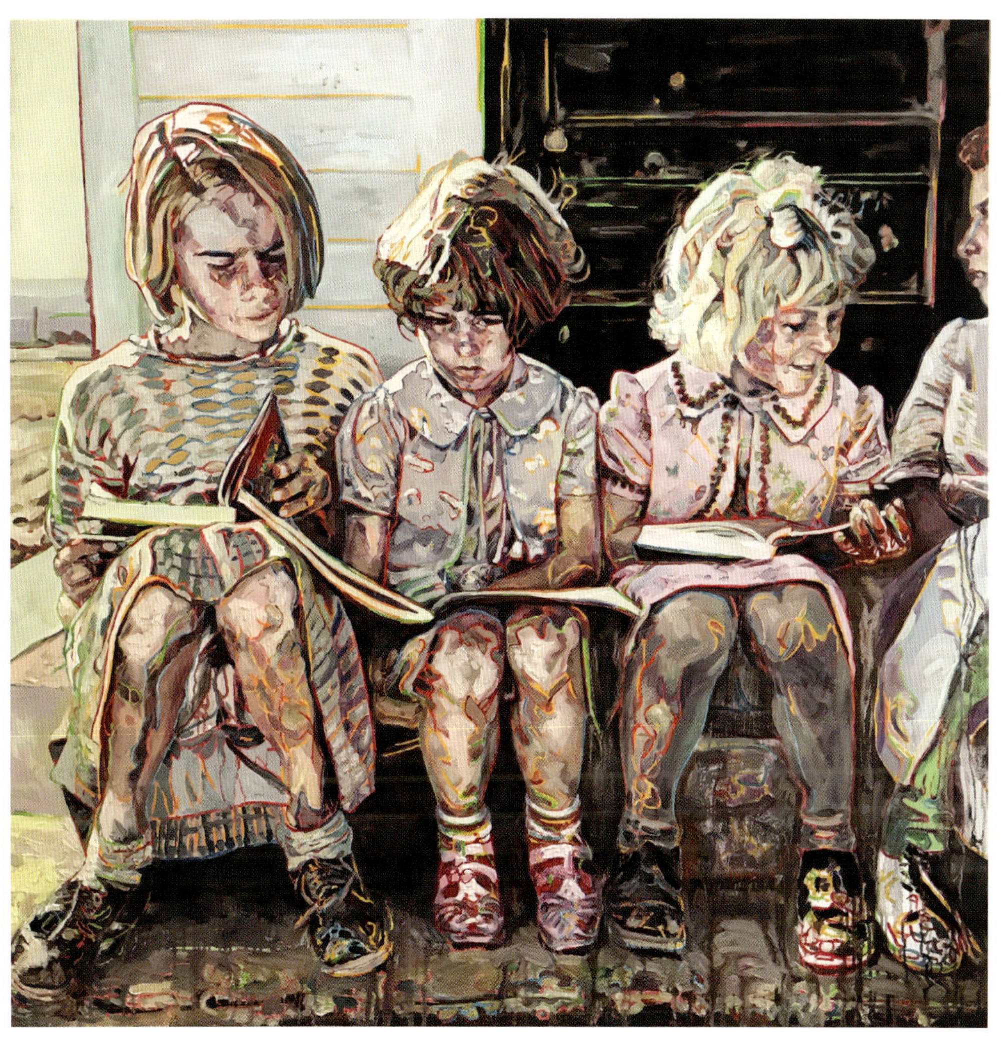

Readers | 2017
oil on canvas | 60 x 60 inches | Private collection

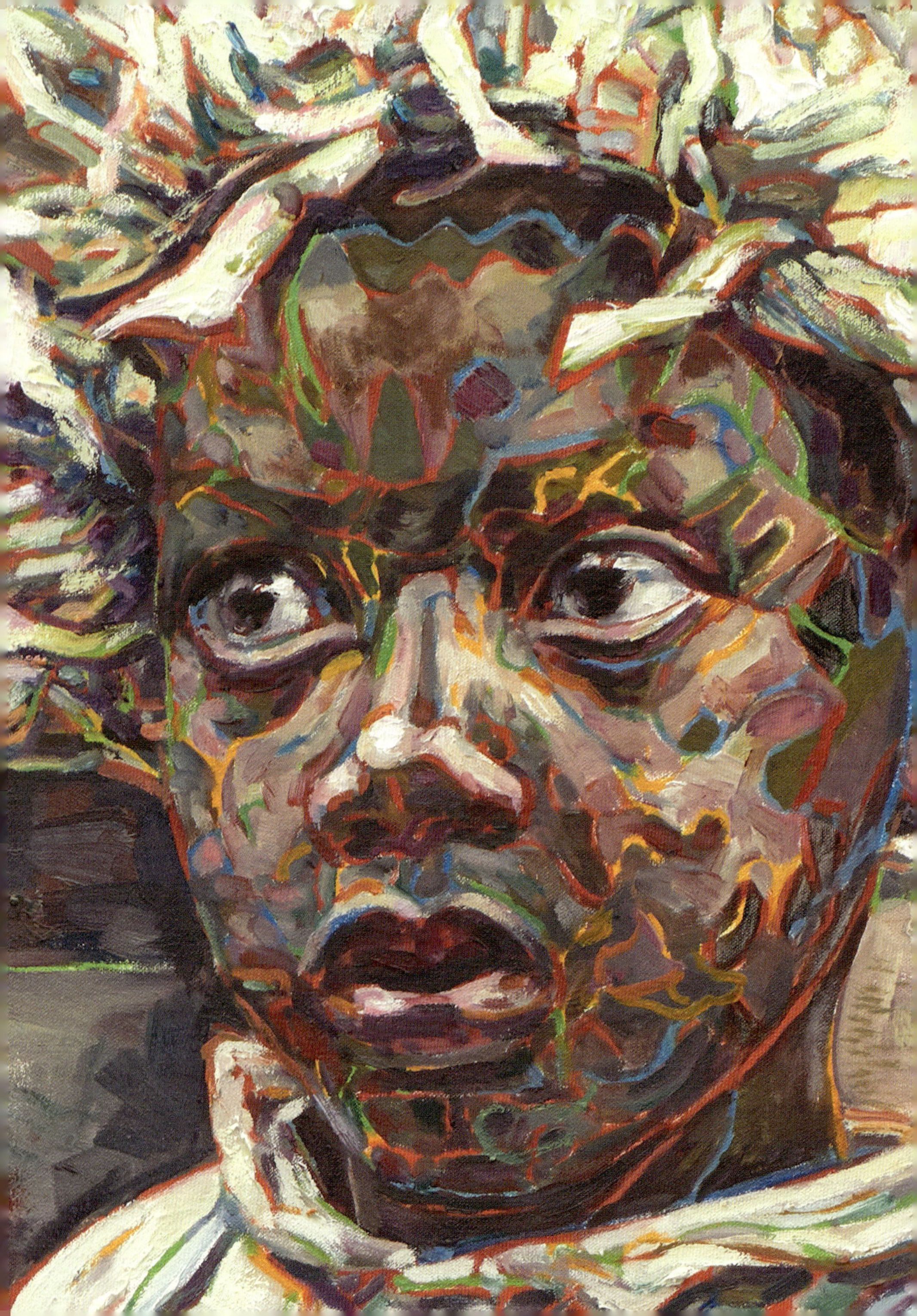

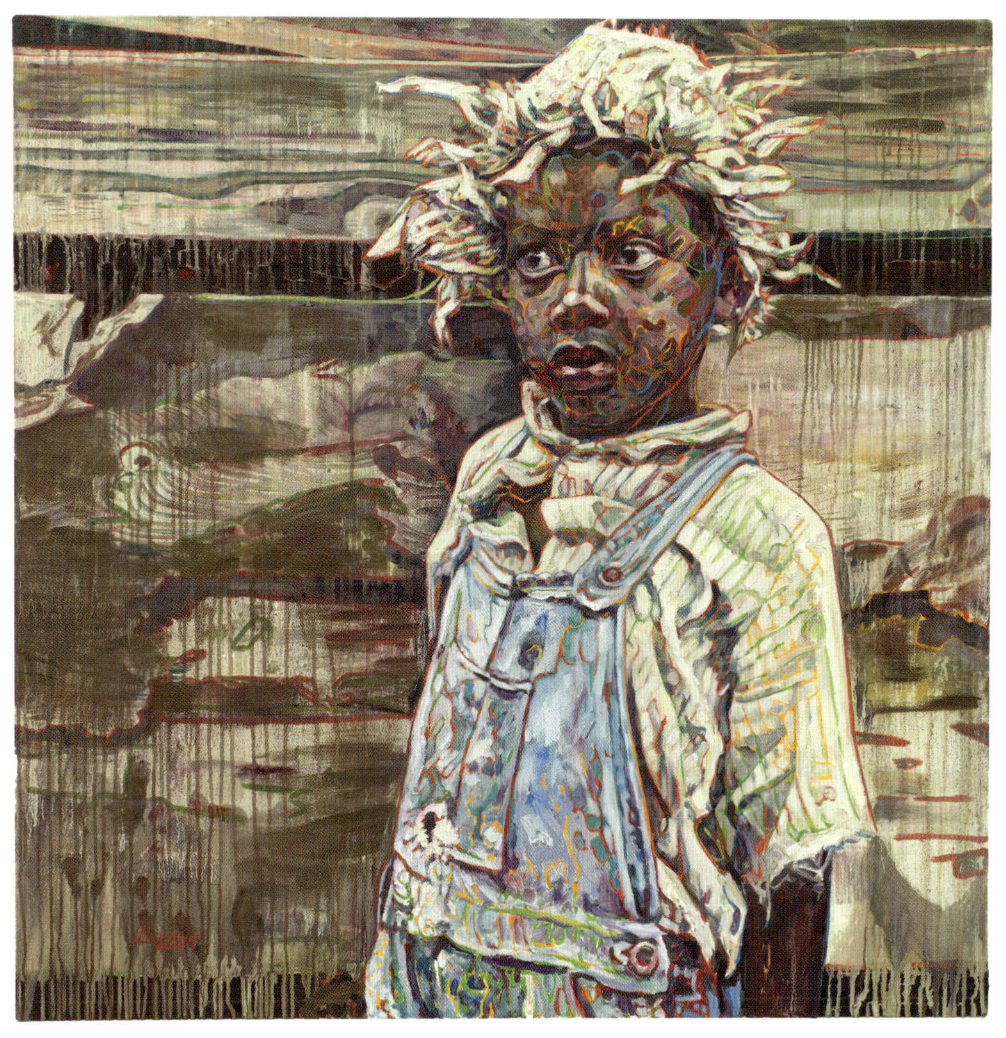

From Granville County | 2017
oil on canvas | 48 x 48 inches | Private collection

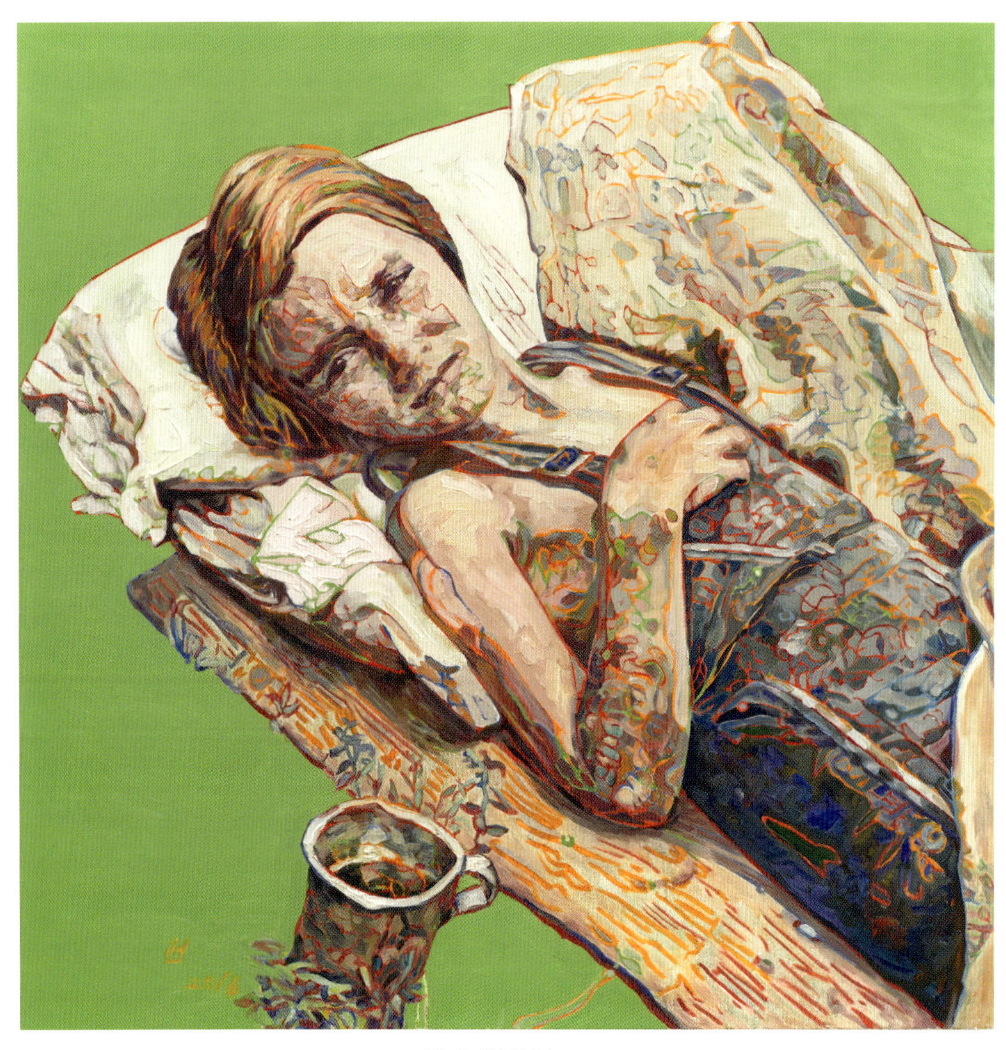

Sick Child | 2018
oil on canvas | 48 x 48 inches | Private collection

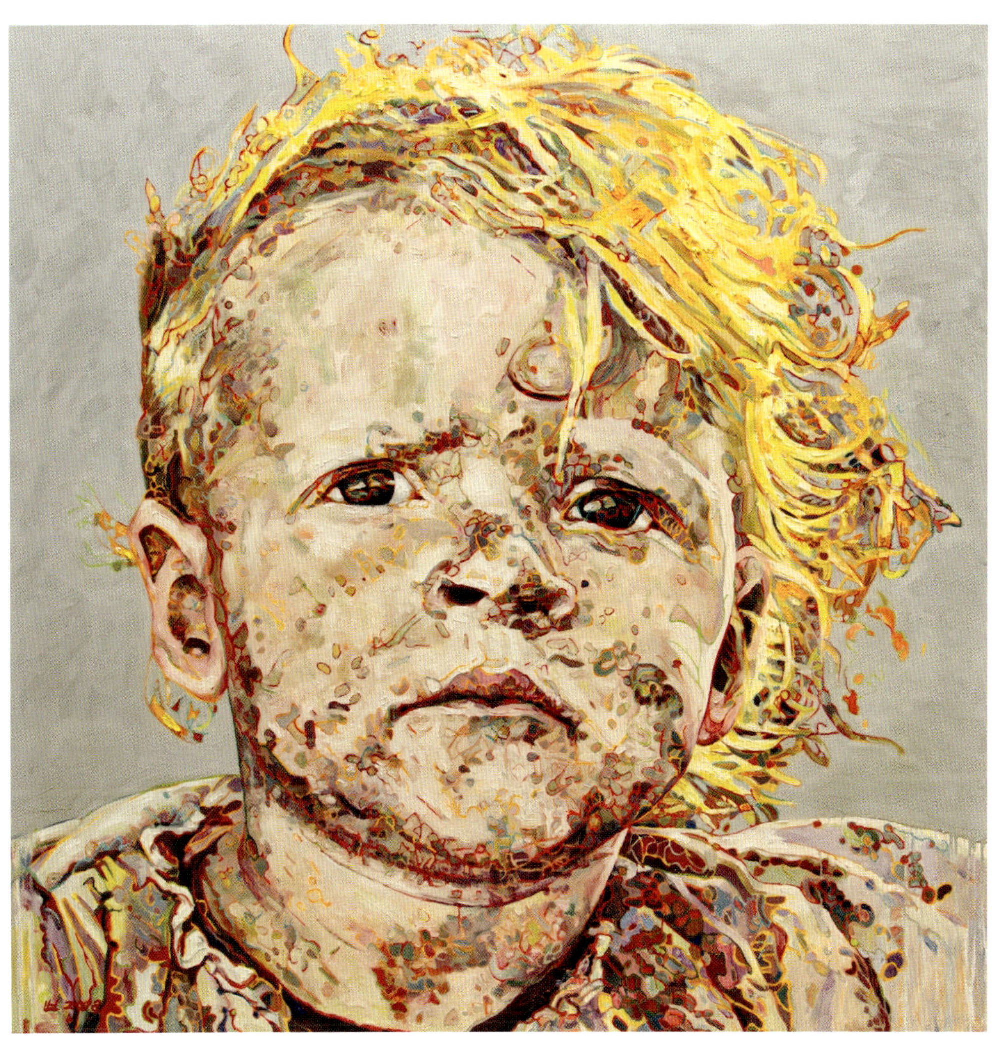

Towhead | 2018
oil on canvas | 72 x 72 inches | Private collection

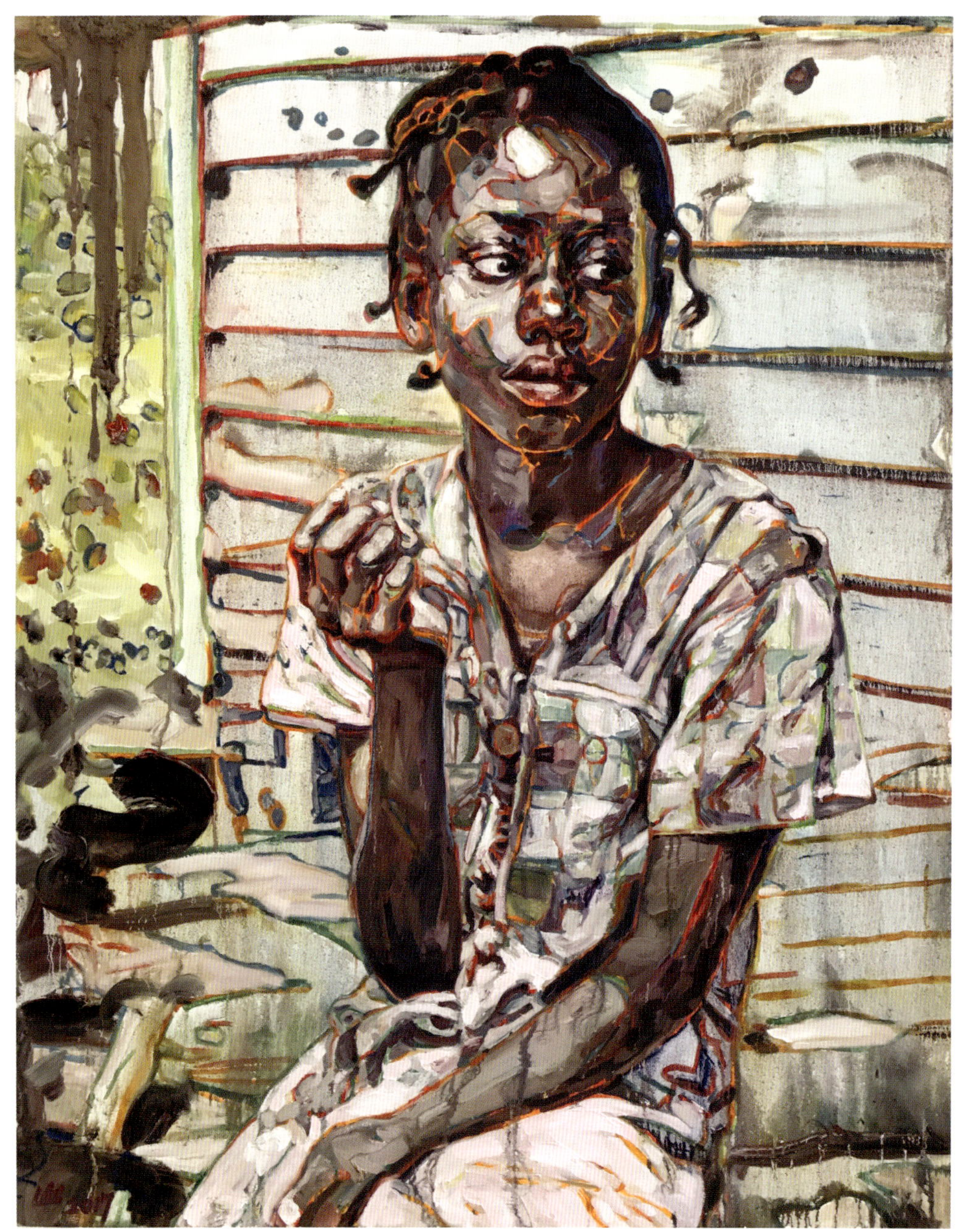

South | 2017
oil on canvas | 60 x 48 inches | Private collection

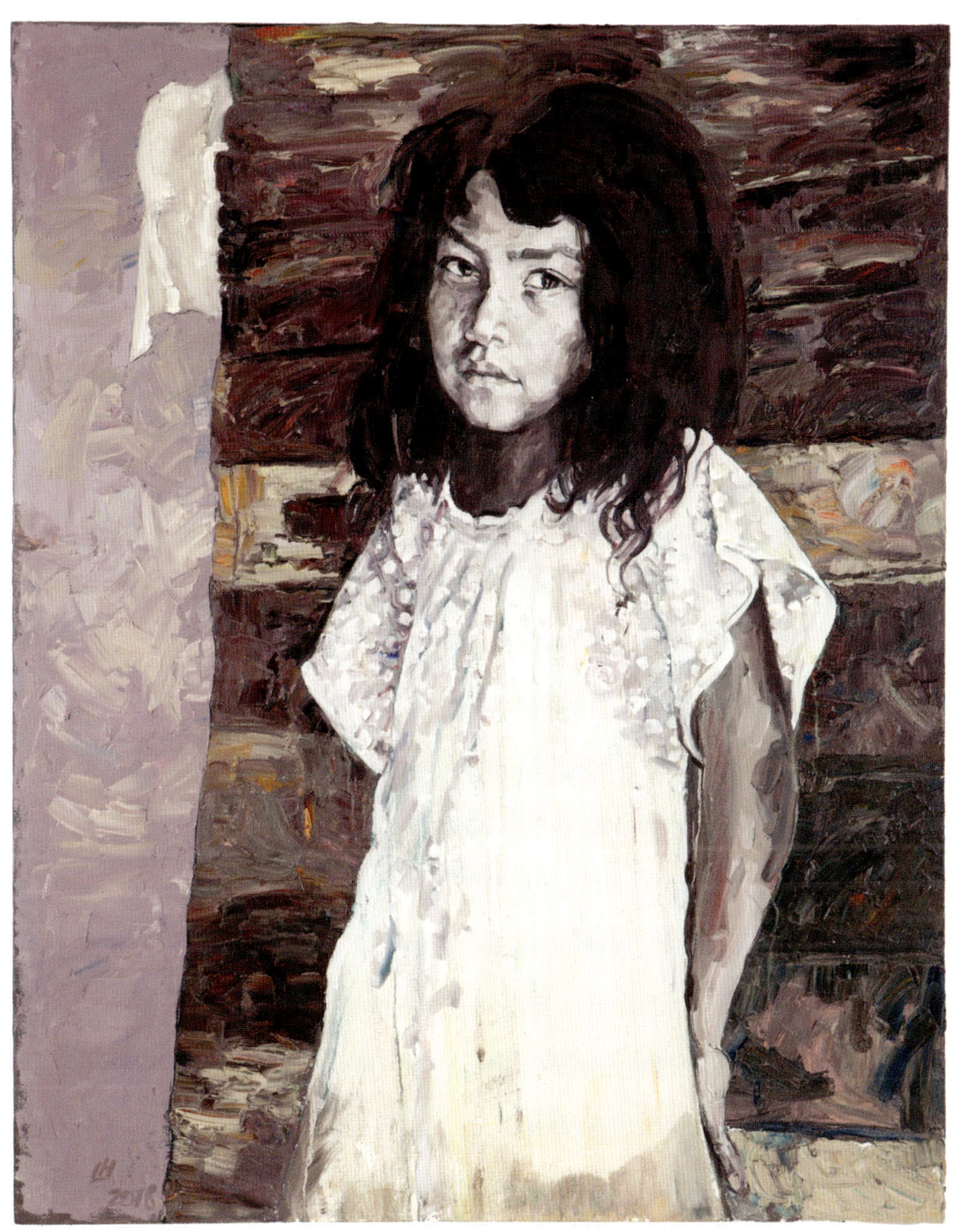

Angel Wing | 2015

oil on canvas | 60 x 48 inches | Collection of the artist

Workers

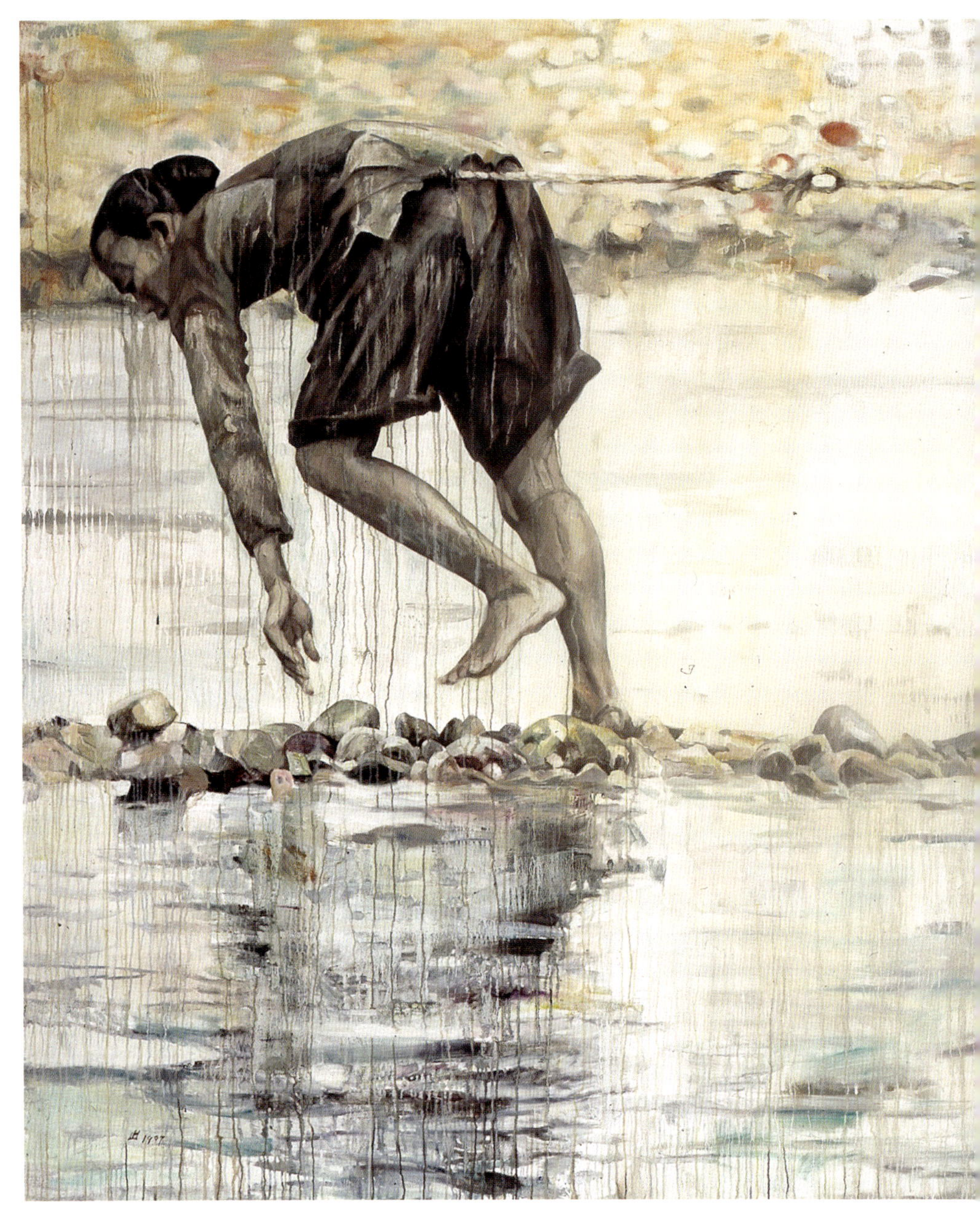

Mu Nu (Mother and Daughter) | 1997

oil on canvas | 80 x 140 inches, diptych | Kemper Museum of Contemporary Art

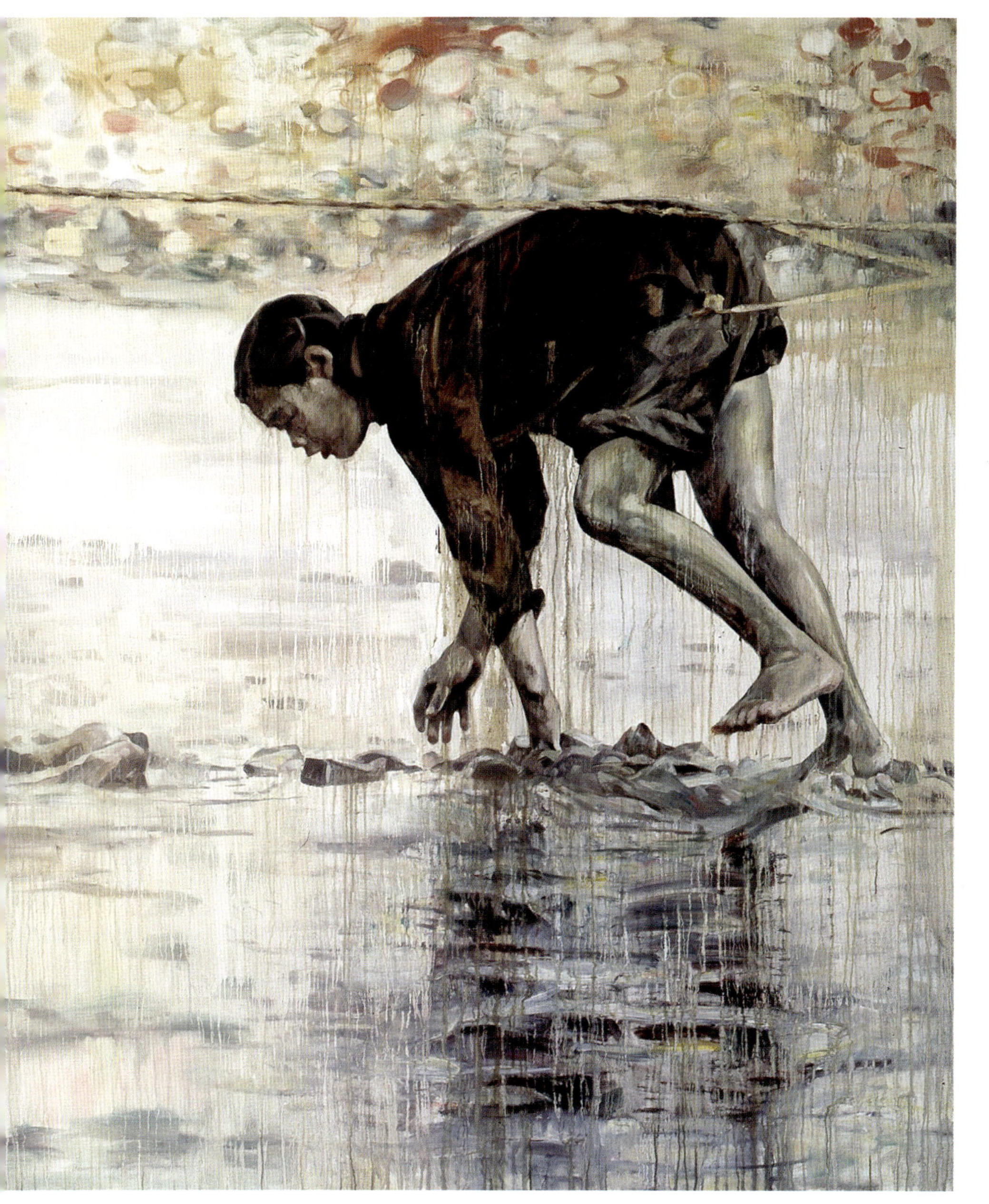

For working people, especially women, there is no rest. The work can never be completed— in a day, in a year, in a generation. It goes on through time, as infants turn into ancestors, and all become ghosts.

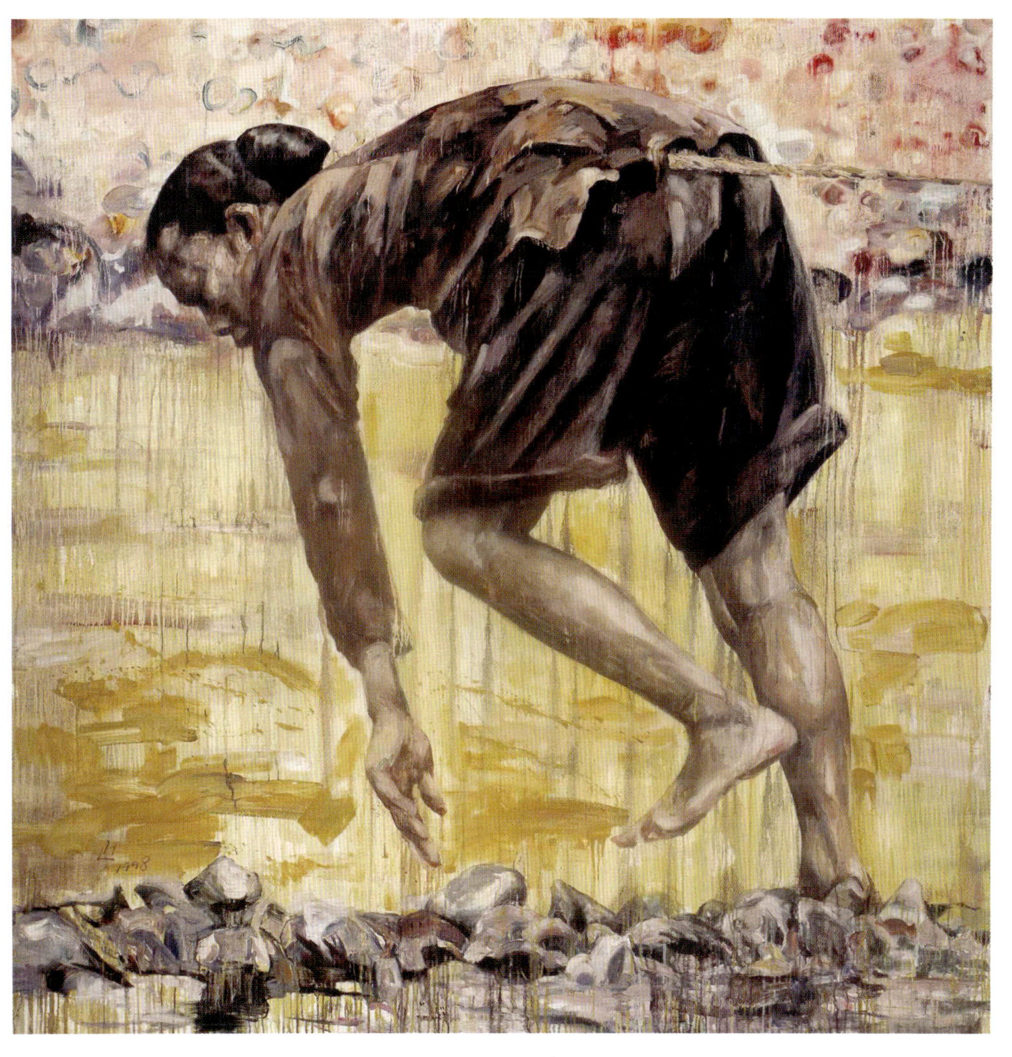

Yellow River | 1997

oil on canvas | 80 x 80 inches | Private collection

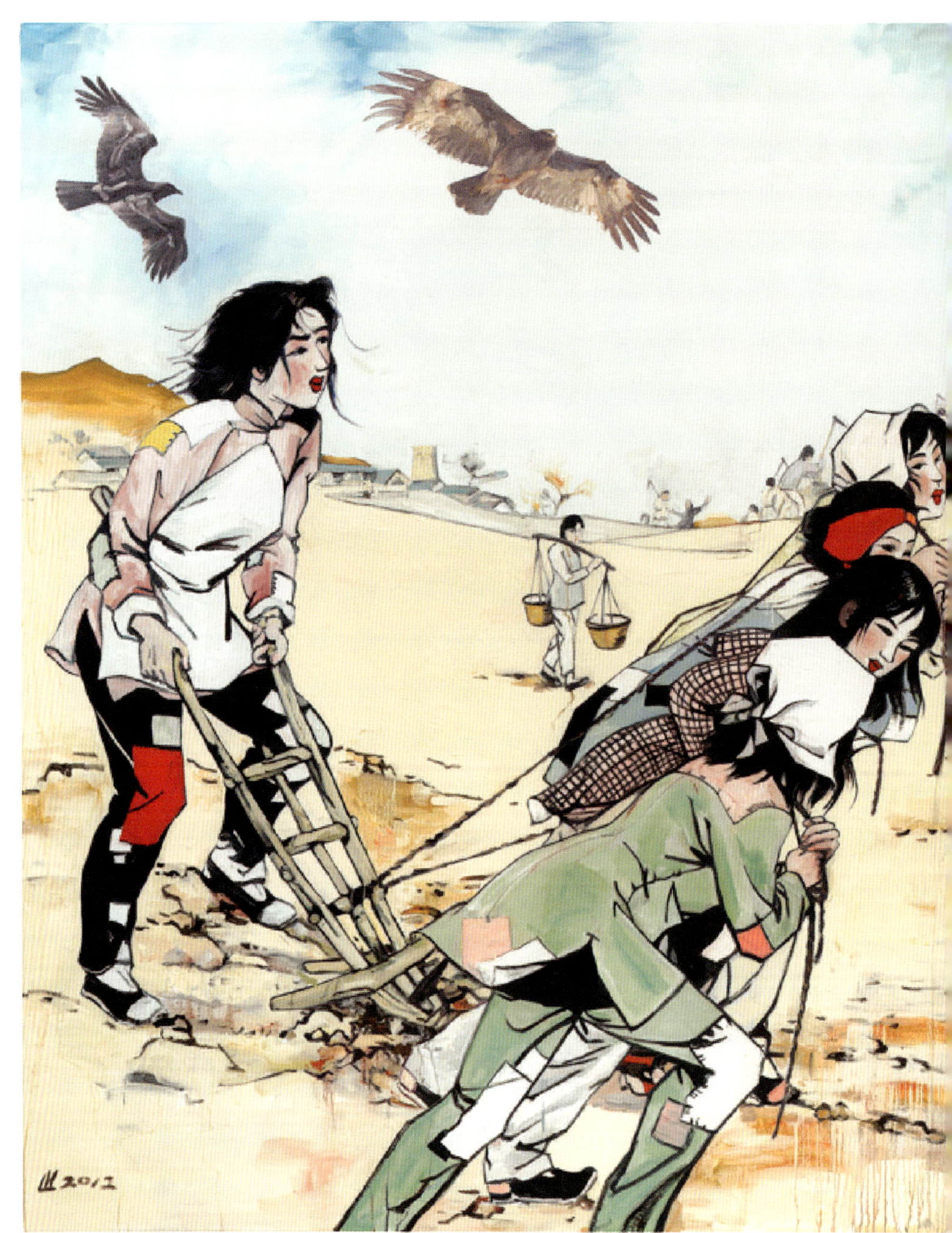

The Heroines | 2012

oil on canvas | 96 x 160 inches | Oakland Museum of California

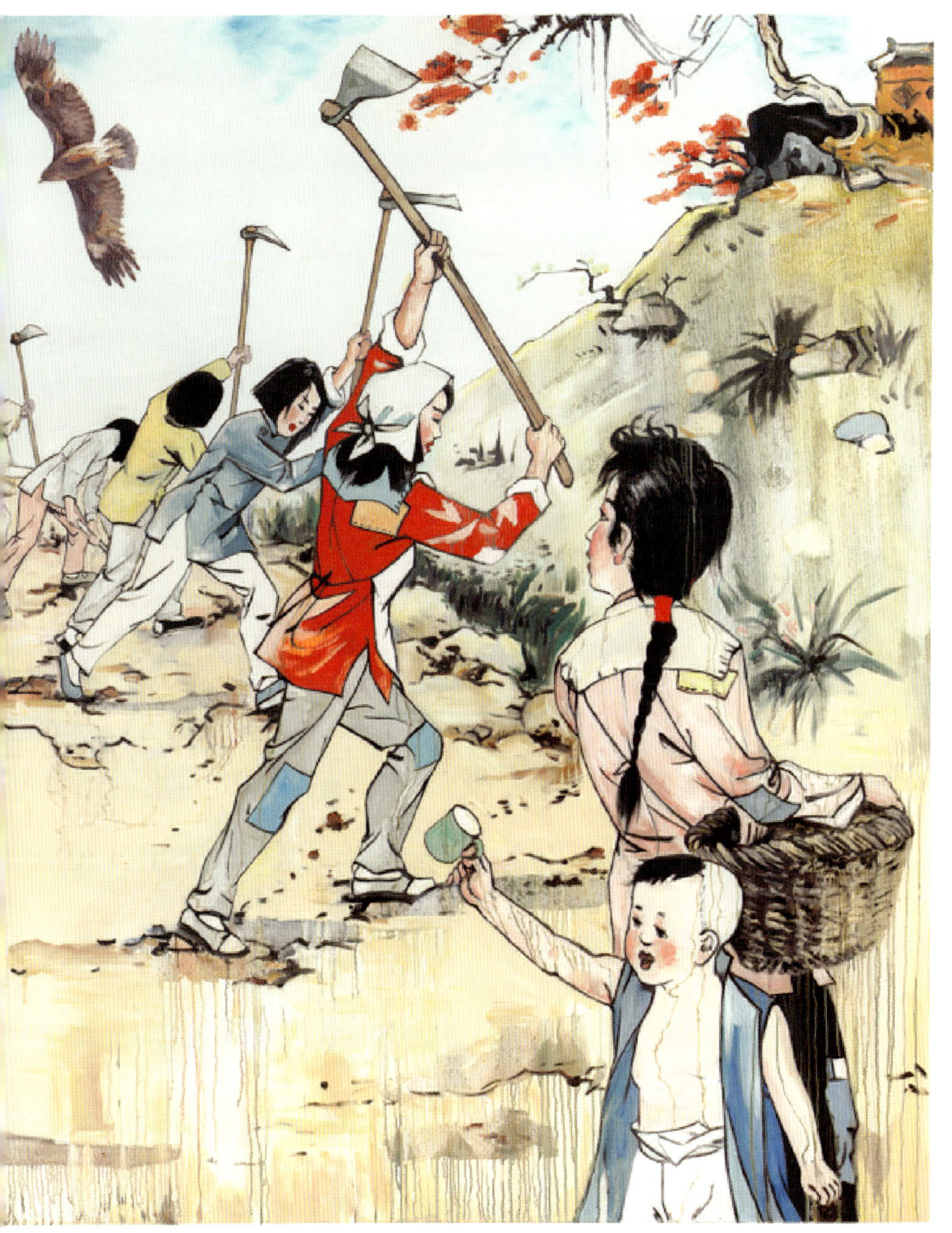

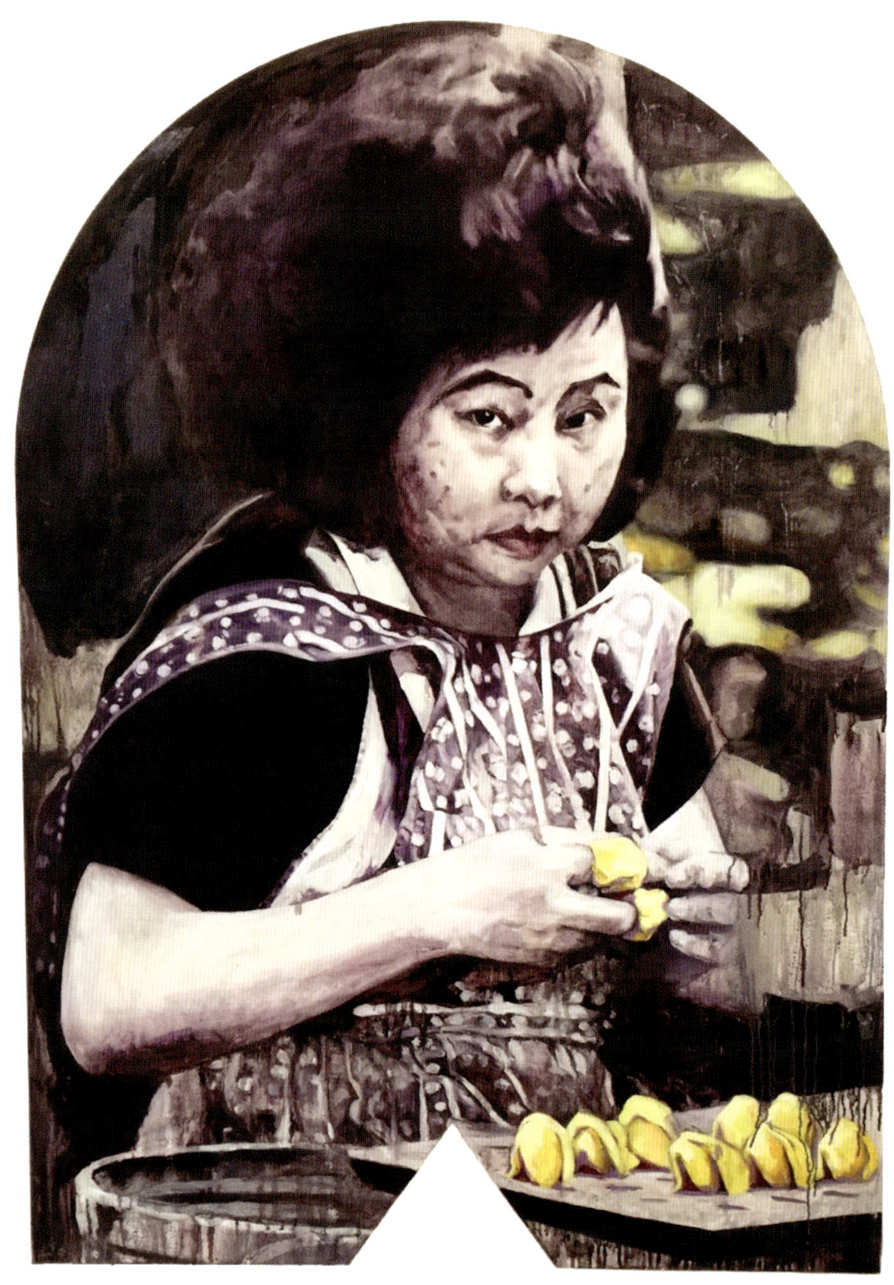

Cookie Queen | 1994
oil on canvas | 67 x 48 inches | Collection of the artist

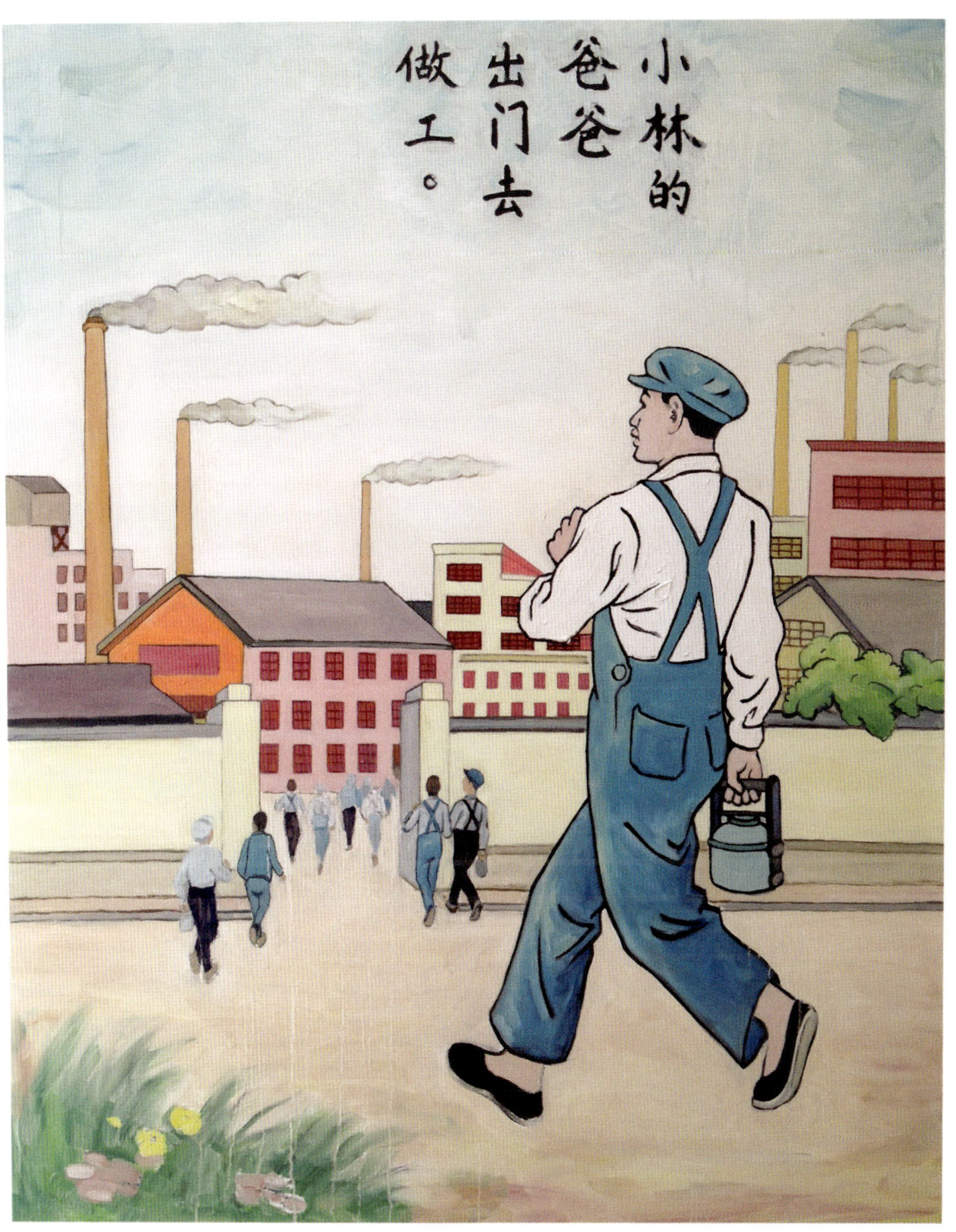

Happy and Gay II | 2012

oil on canvas | 60 x 48 inches | Collection of the artist

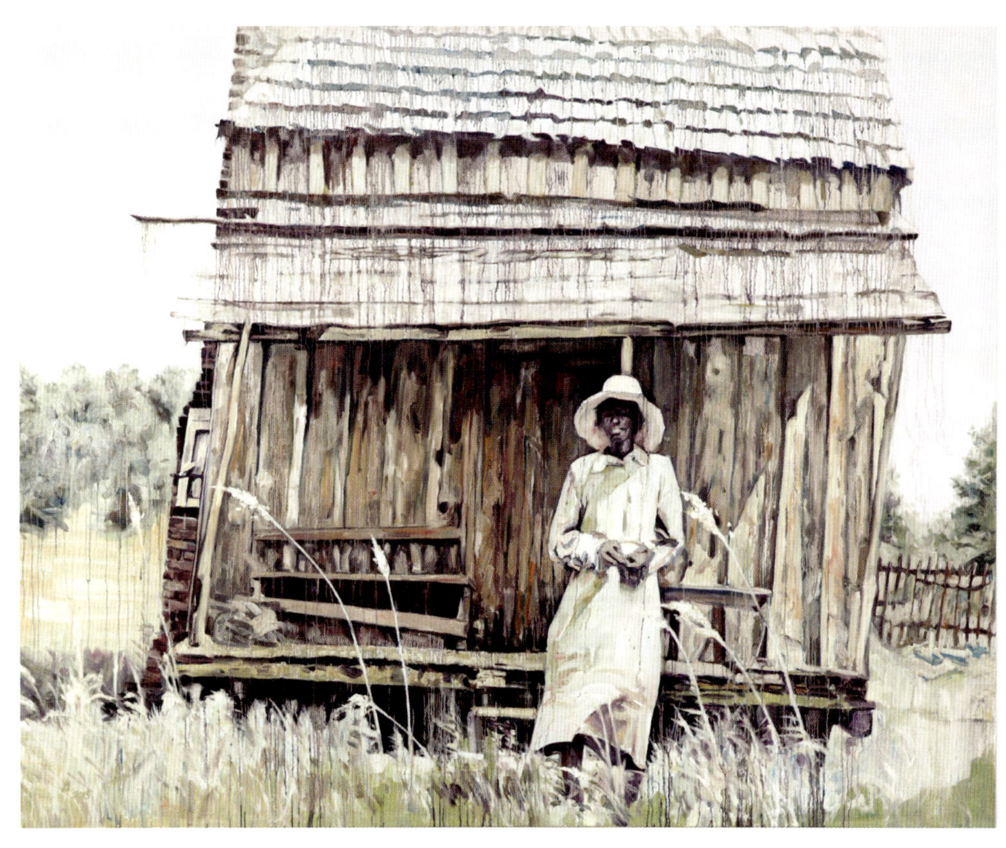

Sharecropper | 2015
oil on canvas | 96 x 120 inches | Private collection

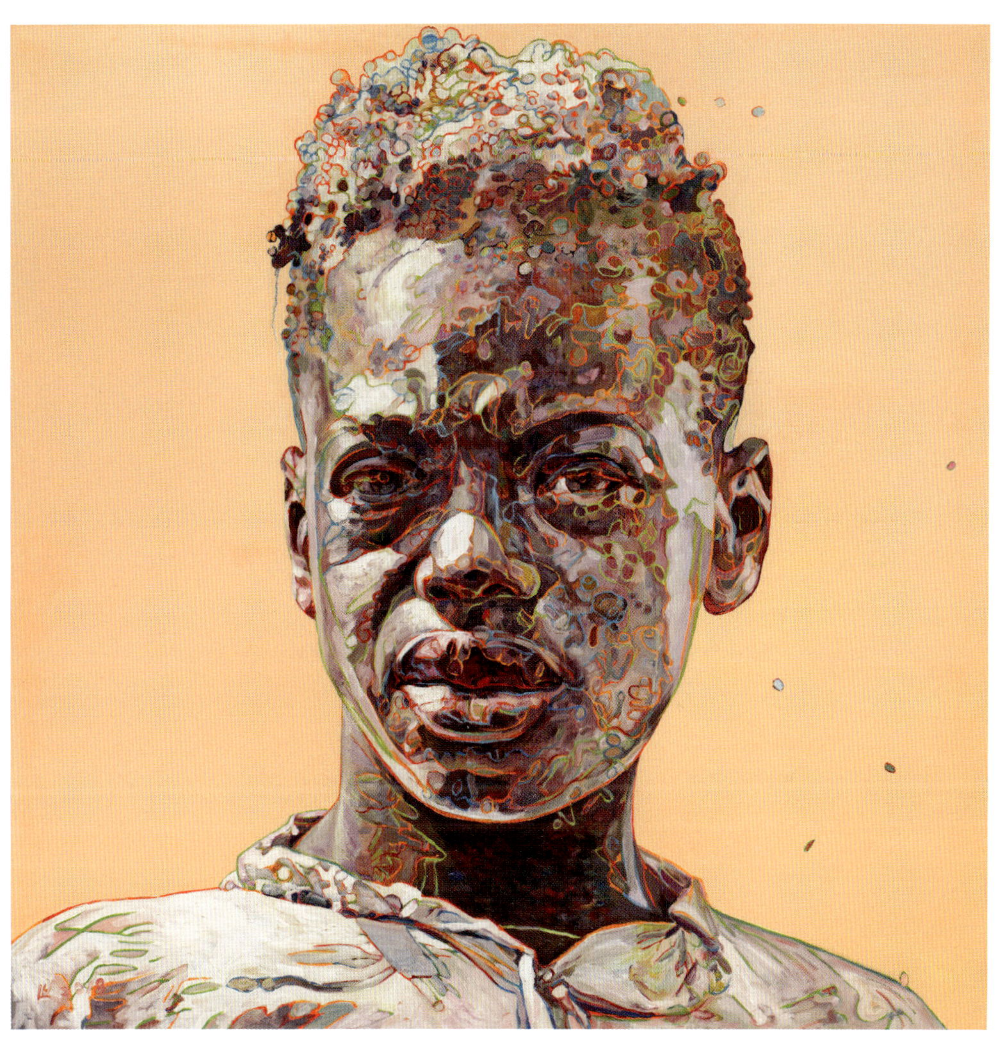

Portrait: Sharecropper | 2018
oil on canvas | 72 x 72 inches | Collection of the artist

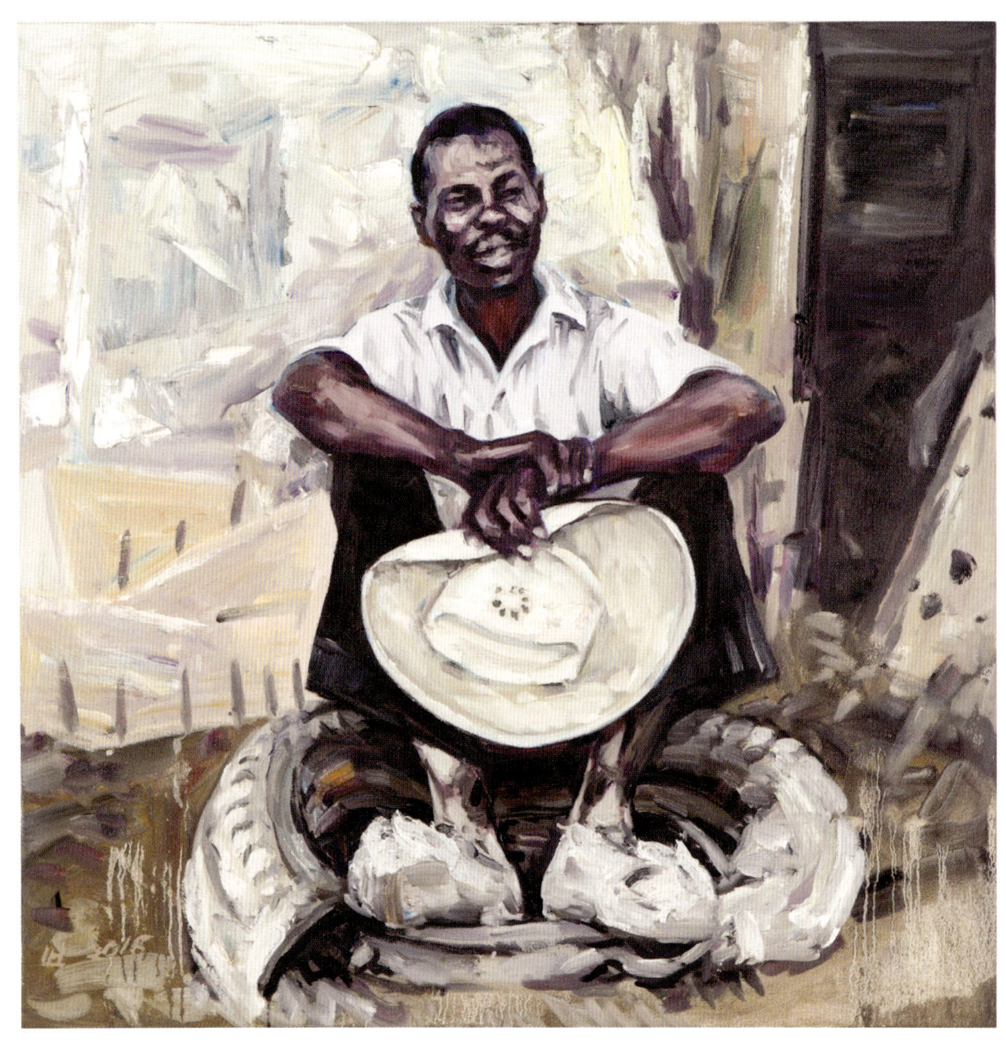

Working Man III | 2016

oil on canvas | 36 x 36 inches | Collection of the artist

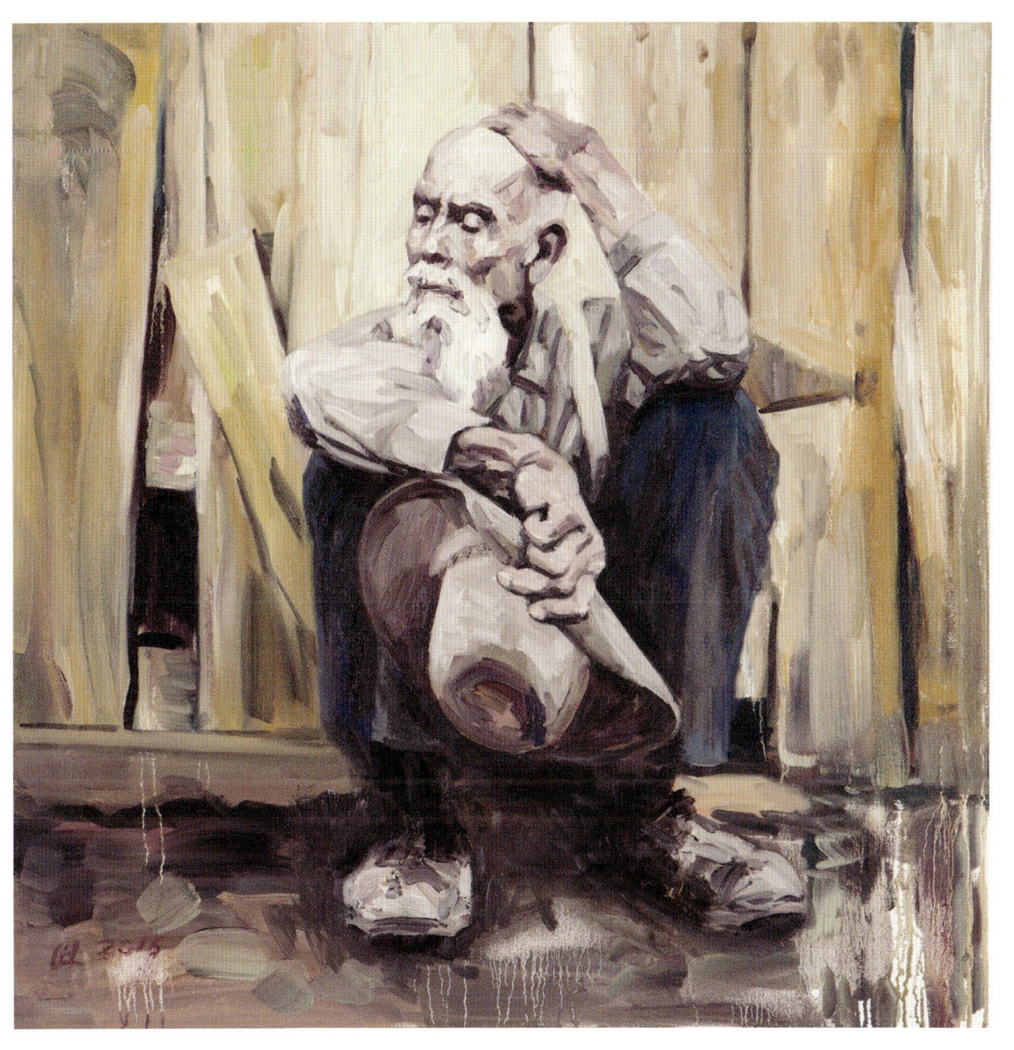

Working Man II | 2016
oil on canvas | 36 x 36 inches | Collection of the artist

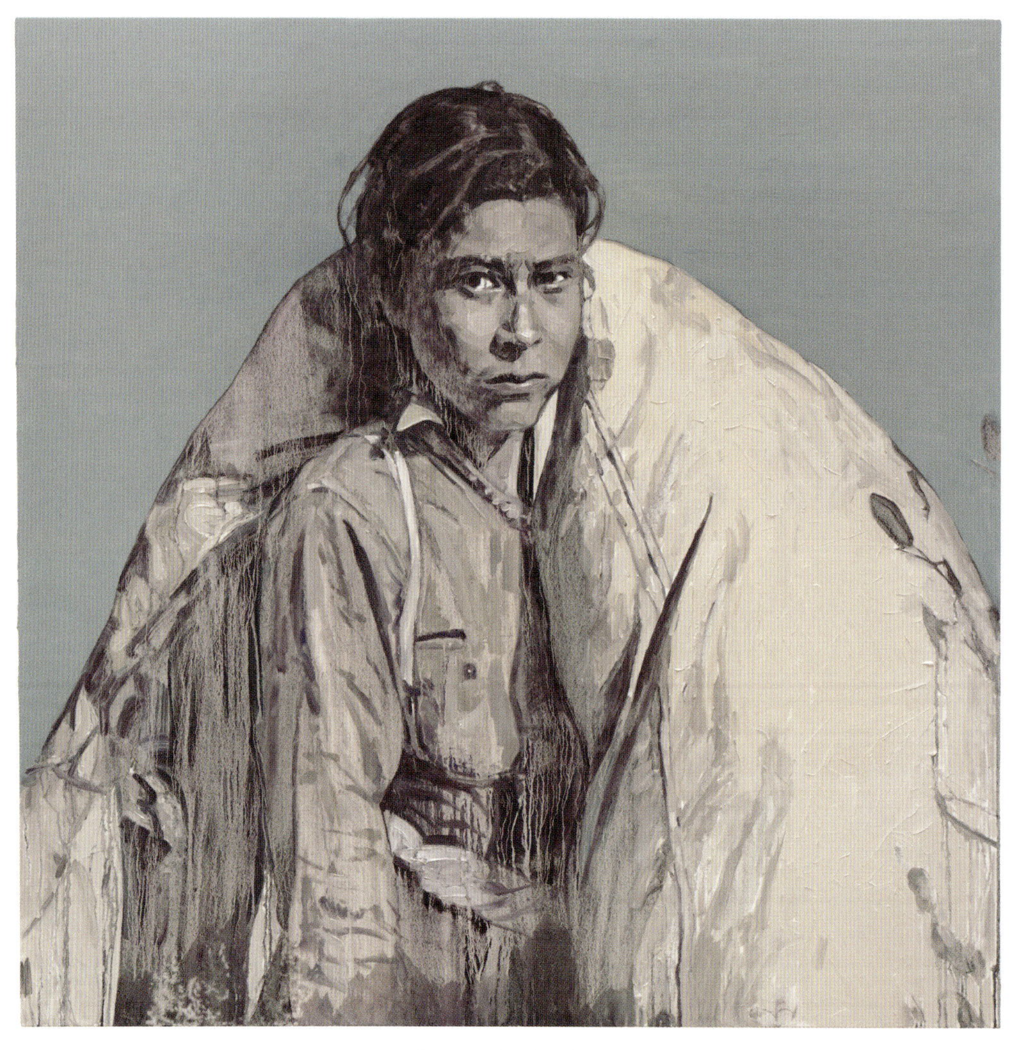

Cotton Picker | 2015
oil on canvas | 66 x 66 inches | Private collection

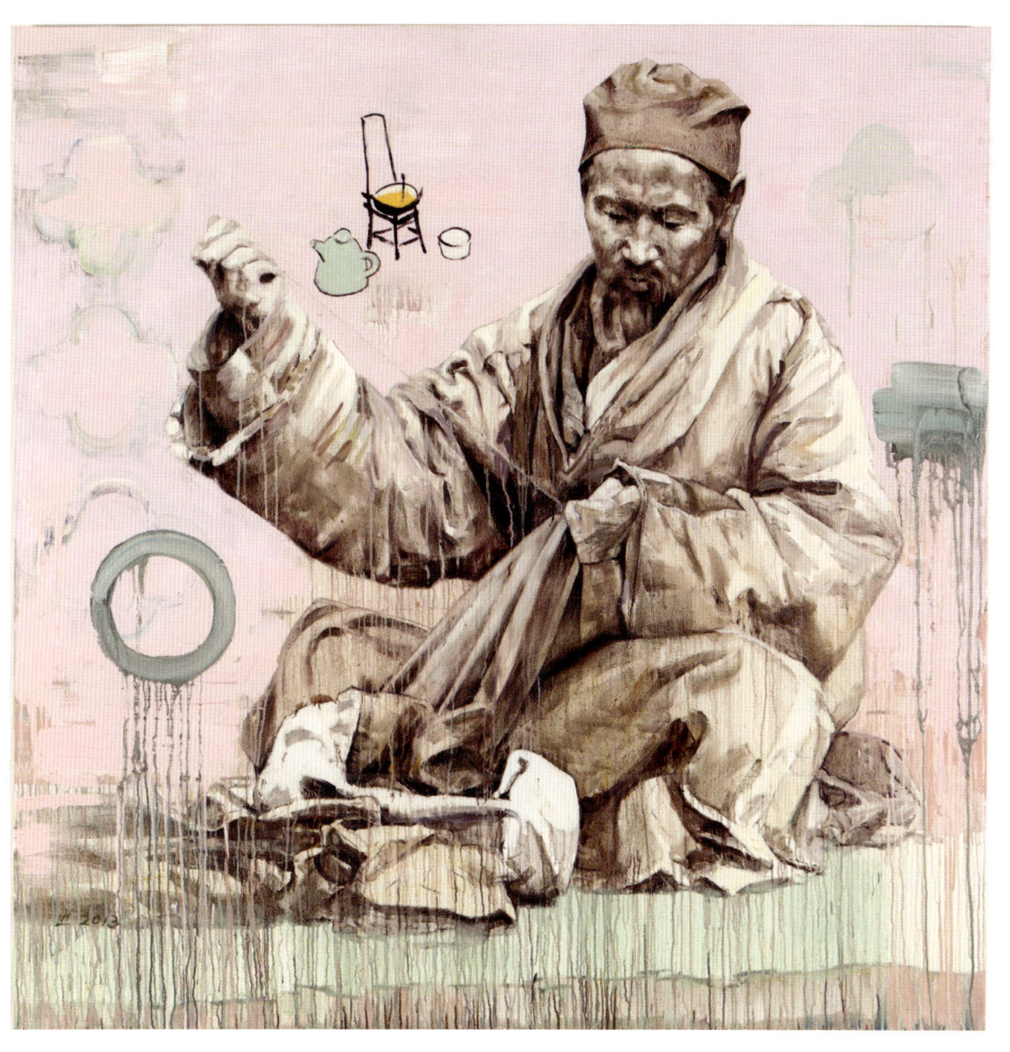

The Sewer | 2013
oil on canvas | 72 x 72 inches | Private collection

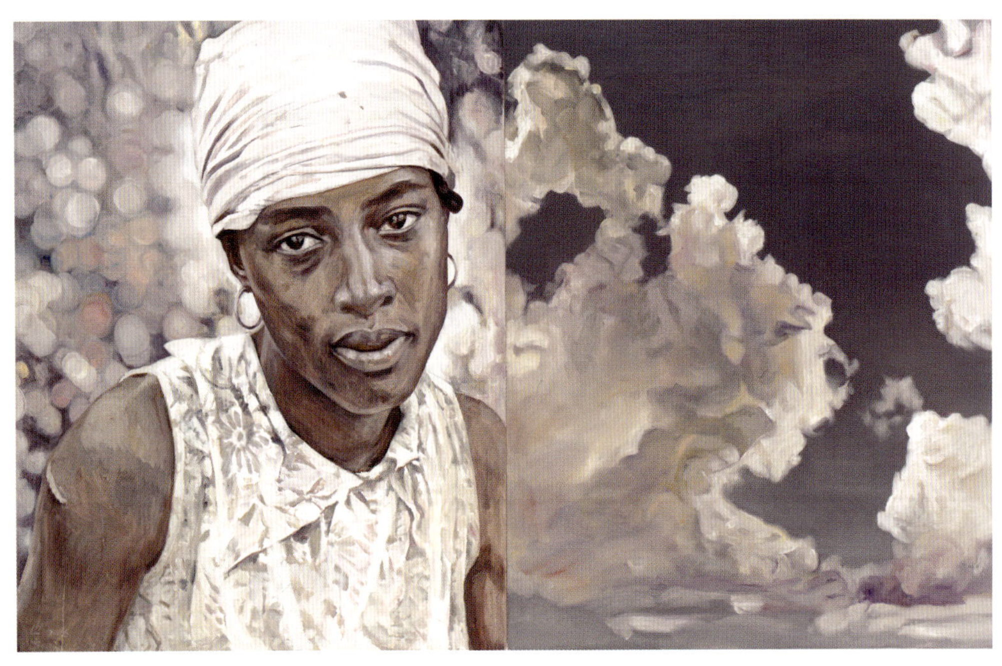

Cotton Hoer, 1936 | 2016

oil on canvas | 60 x 96 inches, diptych | University of Wyoming Art Museum

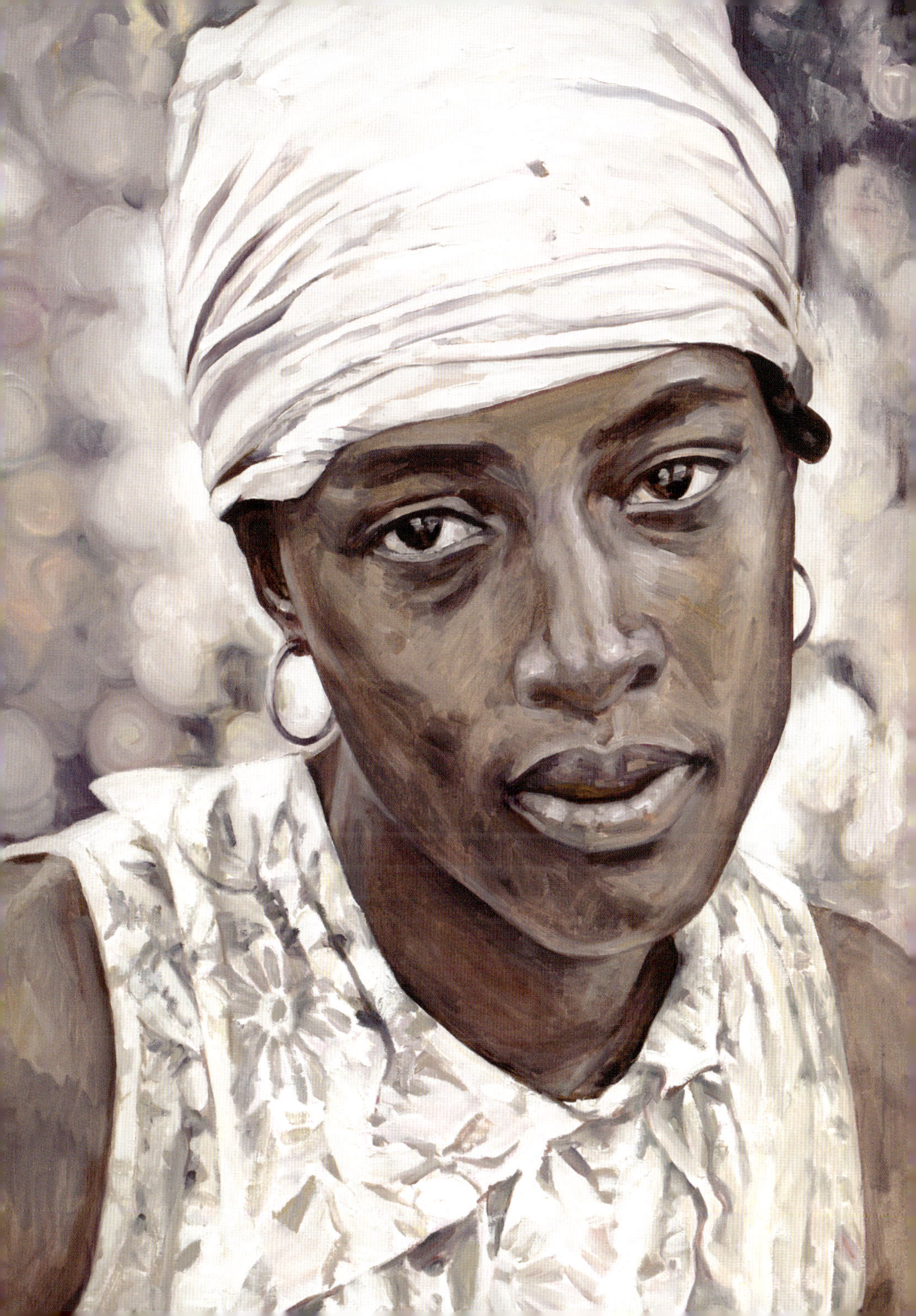

Comfort Women

In the early 1990s I became known for painting images of young Chinese prostitutes based on archival photographs I uncovered during research in Beijing. Because those young women were prostitutes, their photographic images from the late nineteenth and early twentieth century functioned as advertisements, luring male customers. In painting them I tried to bring them back to life by instilling those young women with a certain strength and dignity they don't really have in the photographs. The dignity is in being fully realized as a painting, which returns the viewer's gaze— it looks back at us. The prostitute paintings disrupt the power dynamic between an exotic female image and its Western male viewer.

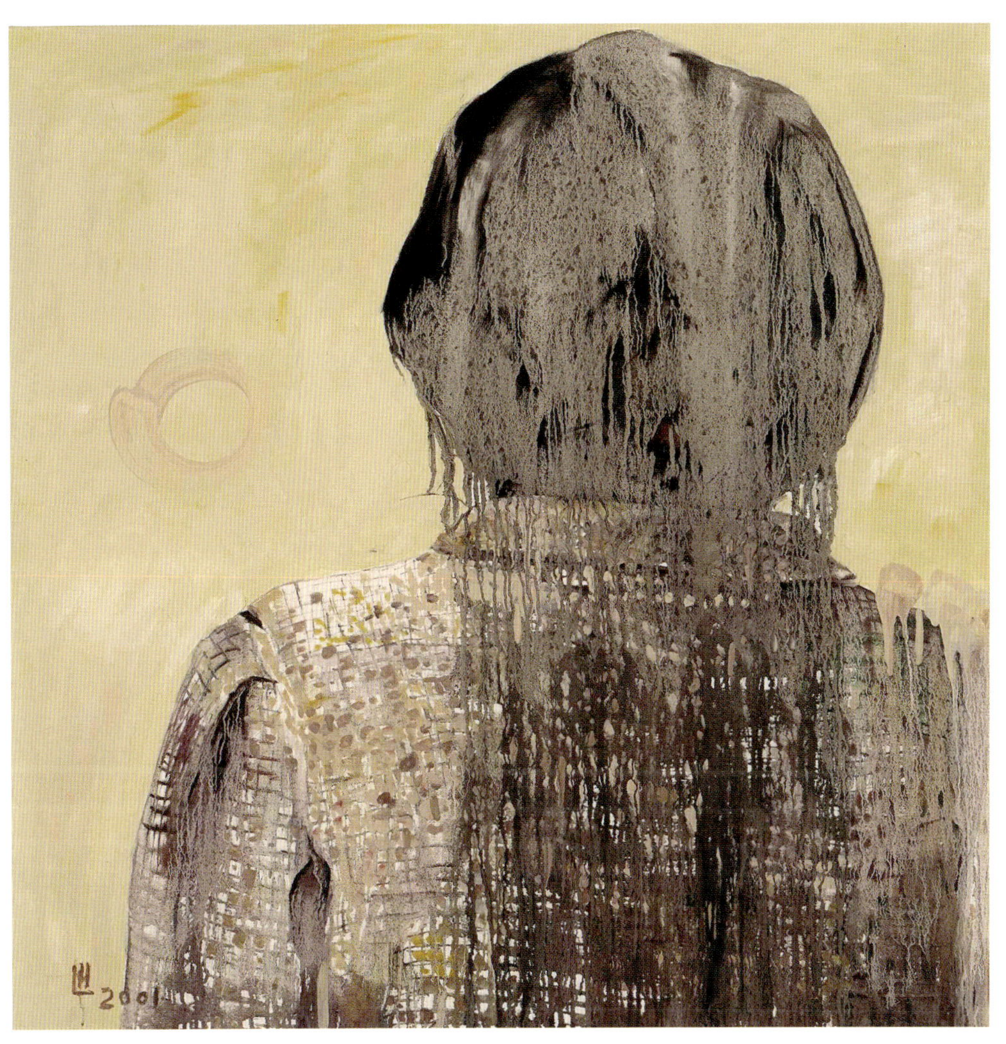

Comfort Women # 1 | 2001

oil on canvas | 36 x 36 inches | Collection of the artist

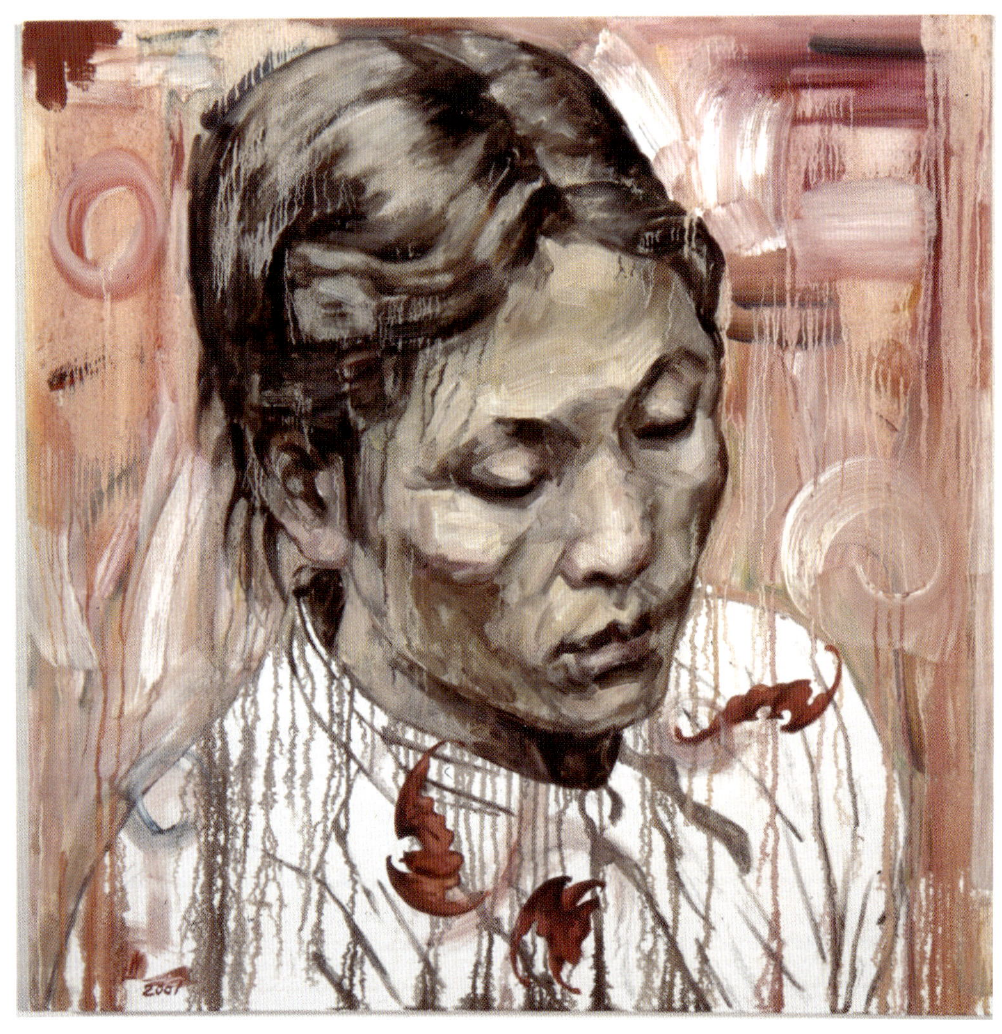

Comfort Women #5 | 2001

oil on canvas | 36 x 36 inches | Private collection

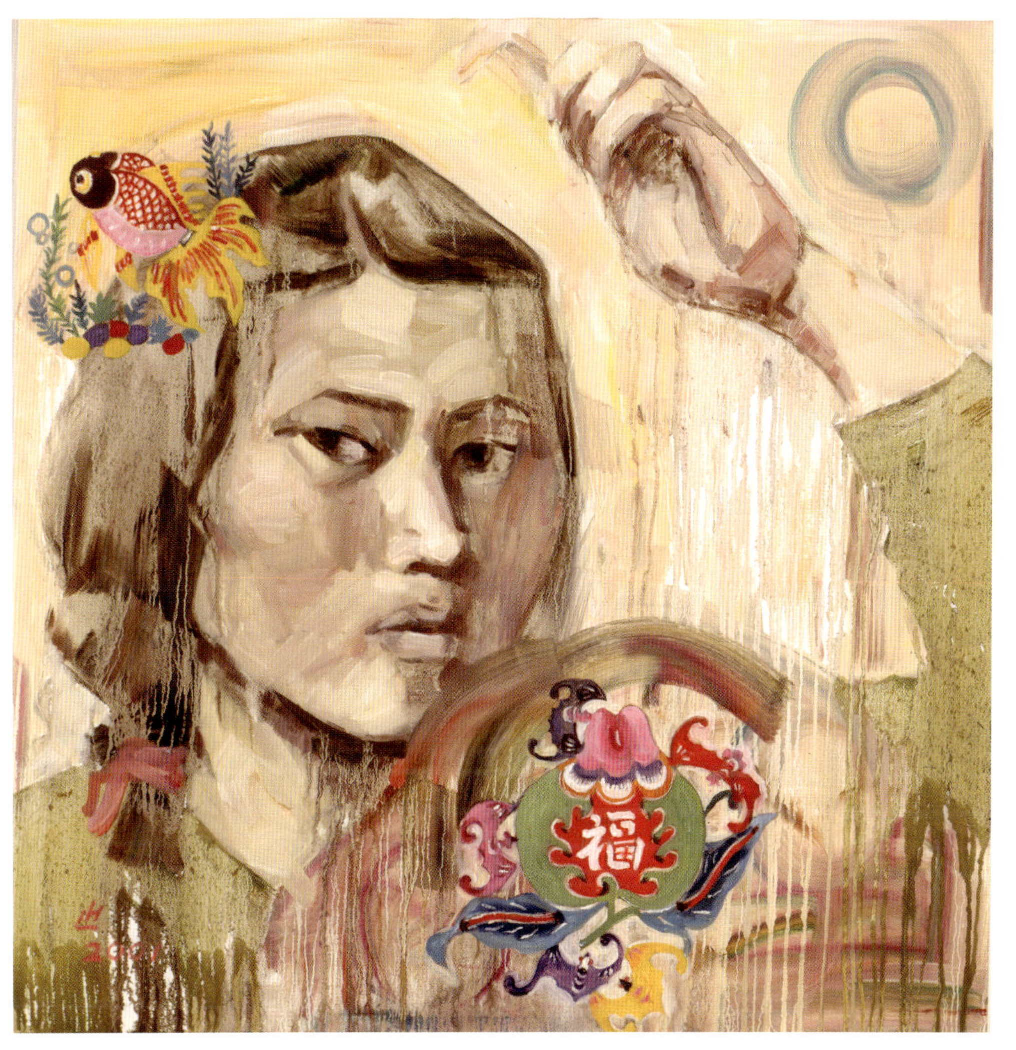

Comfort Women #8 | 2001
oil on canvas | 36 x 36 inches | Private collection

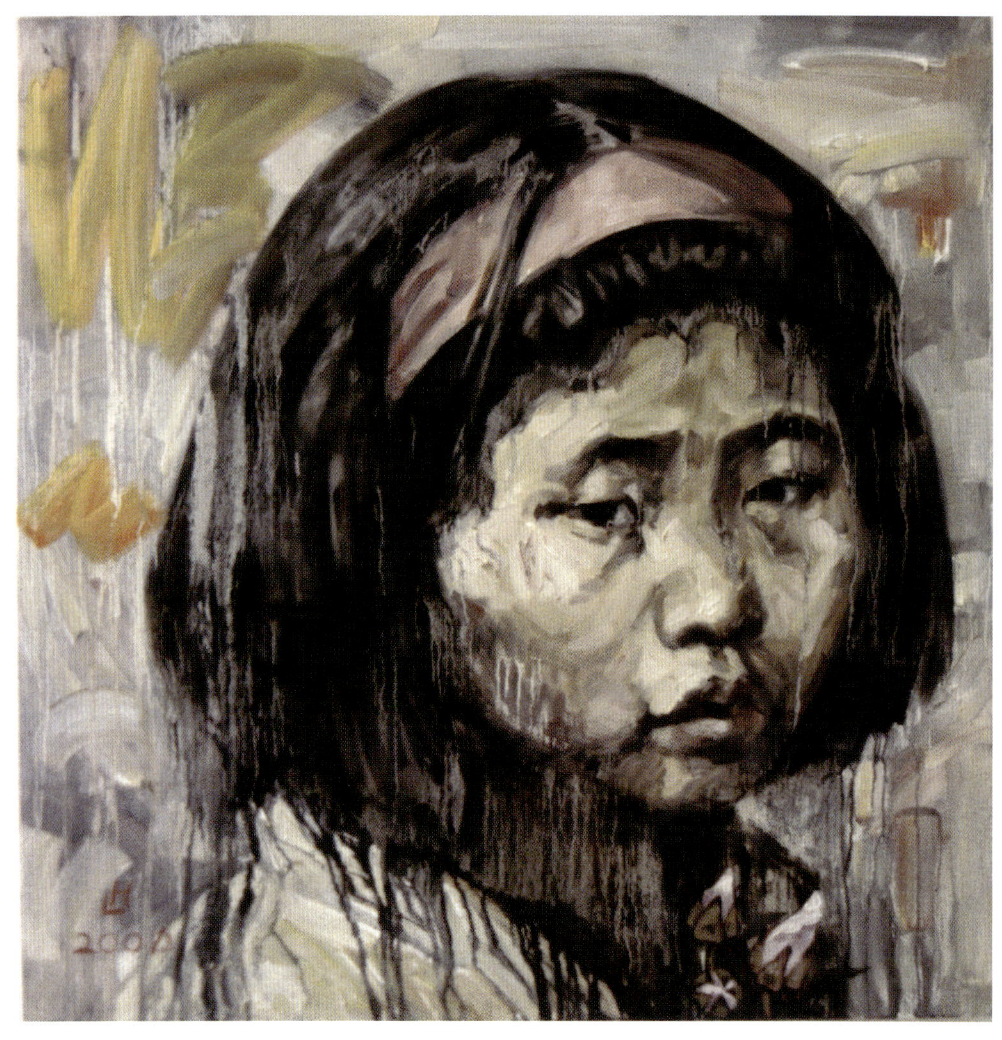

Comfort Women #6 | 2000
oil on canvas | 36 x 36 inches | Private collection

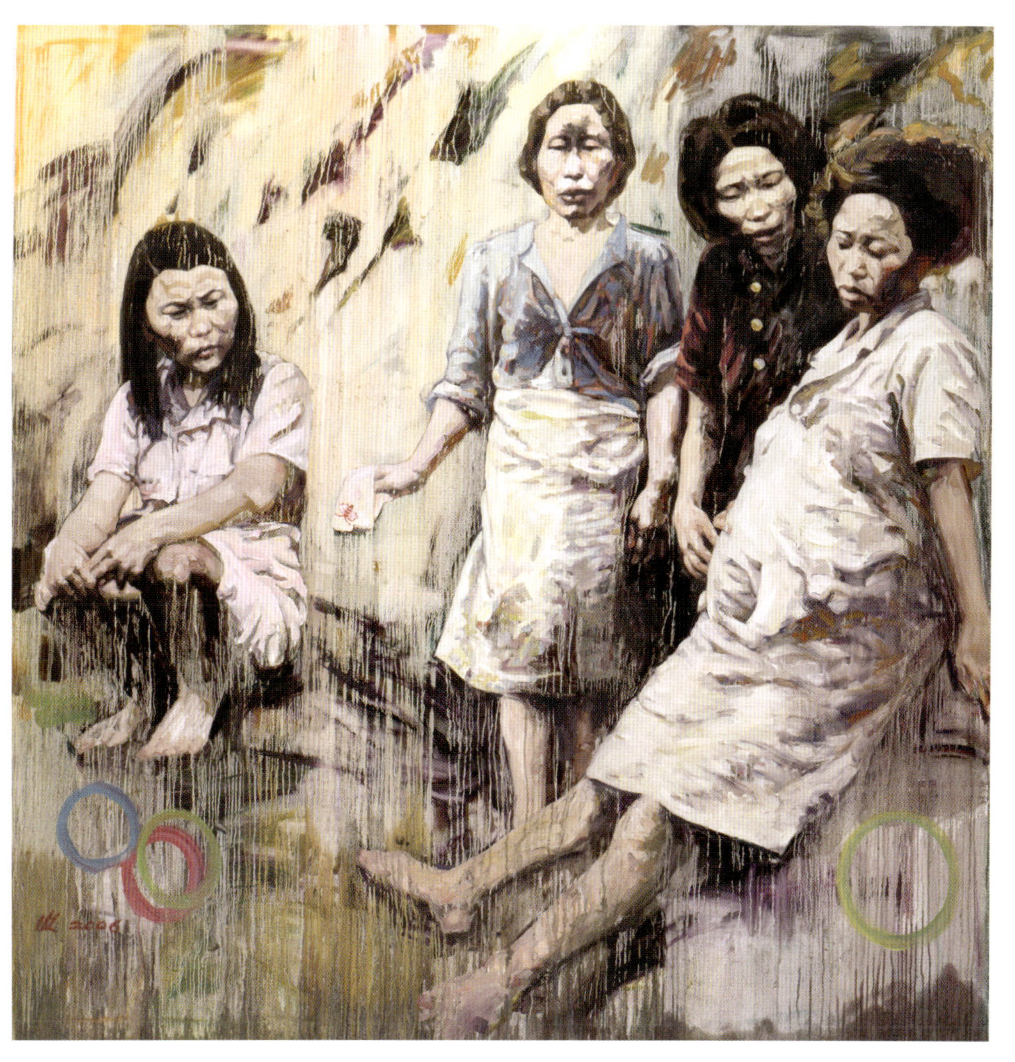

Strange Fruit II (Comfort Women) | 2006
oil on canvas | 80 x 80 inches | Collection of the artist

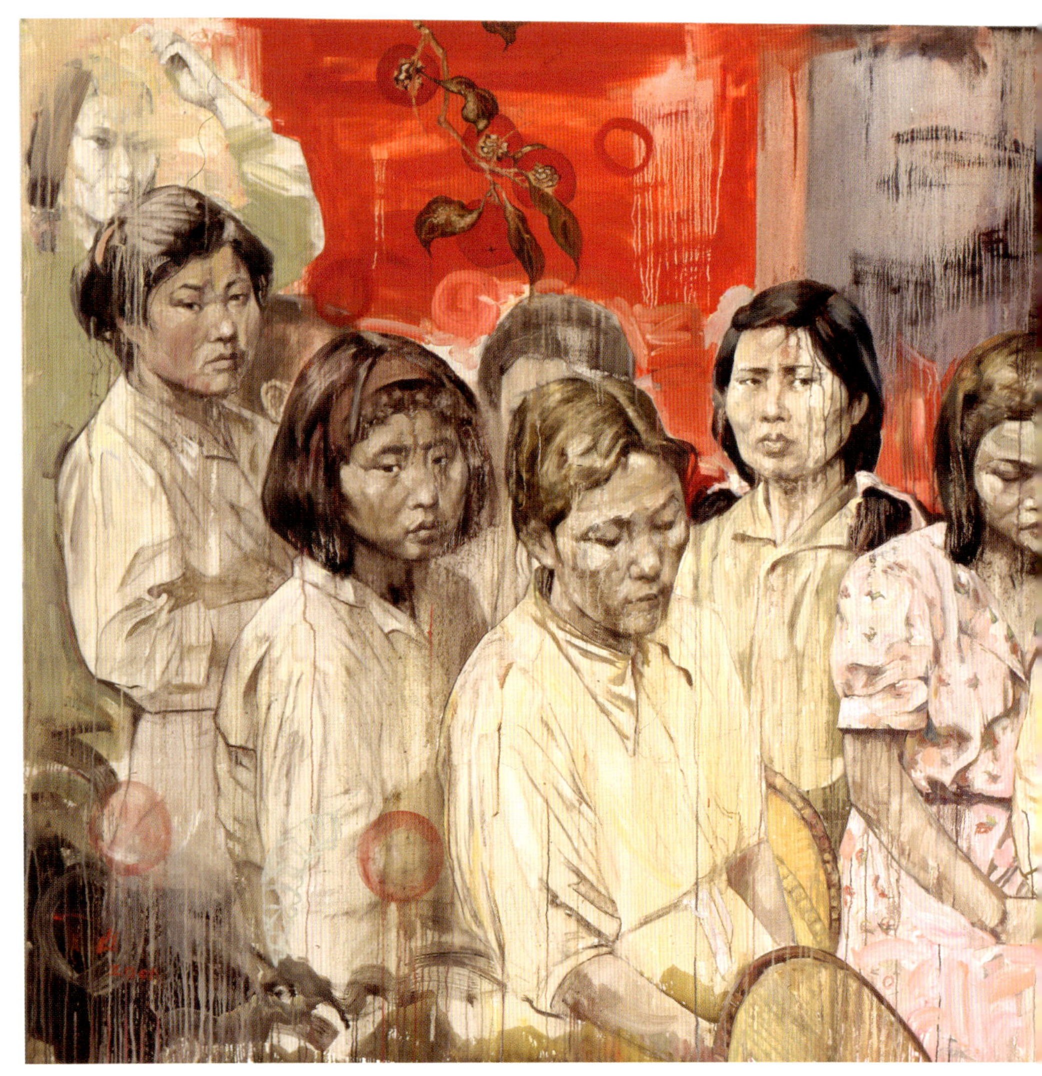

Strange Fruit: Comfort Women | 2001
oil on canvas | 80 x 160 inches | The Karen and Robert Duncan Collection

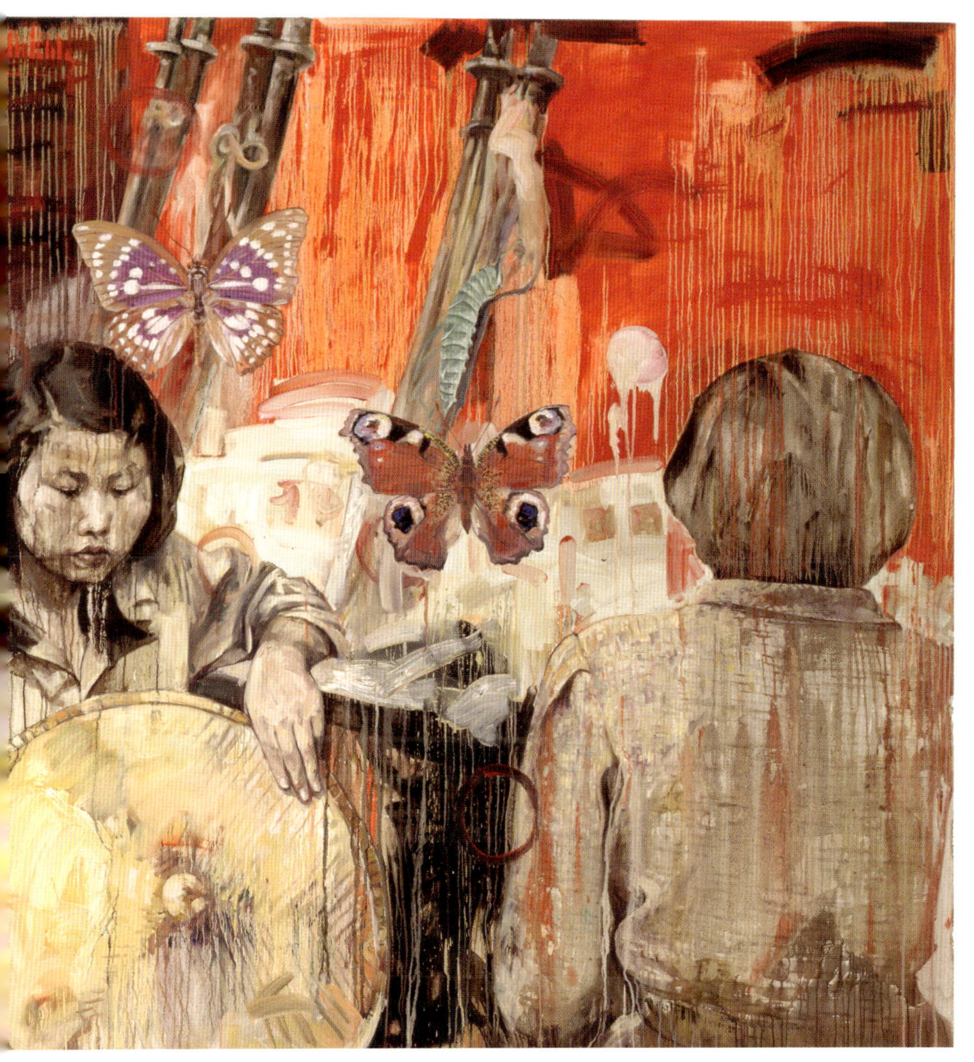

Refugees and Migrants

We are all from somewhere else. Therefore, we are all refugees of some sort, emigrants or immigrants, migrants or émigrés. We carry ourselves, our ancestors' ghosts, to wherever we have gone or are going, and we follow them back as far as their images will take us.

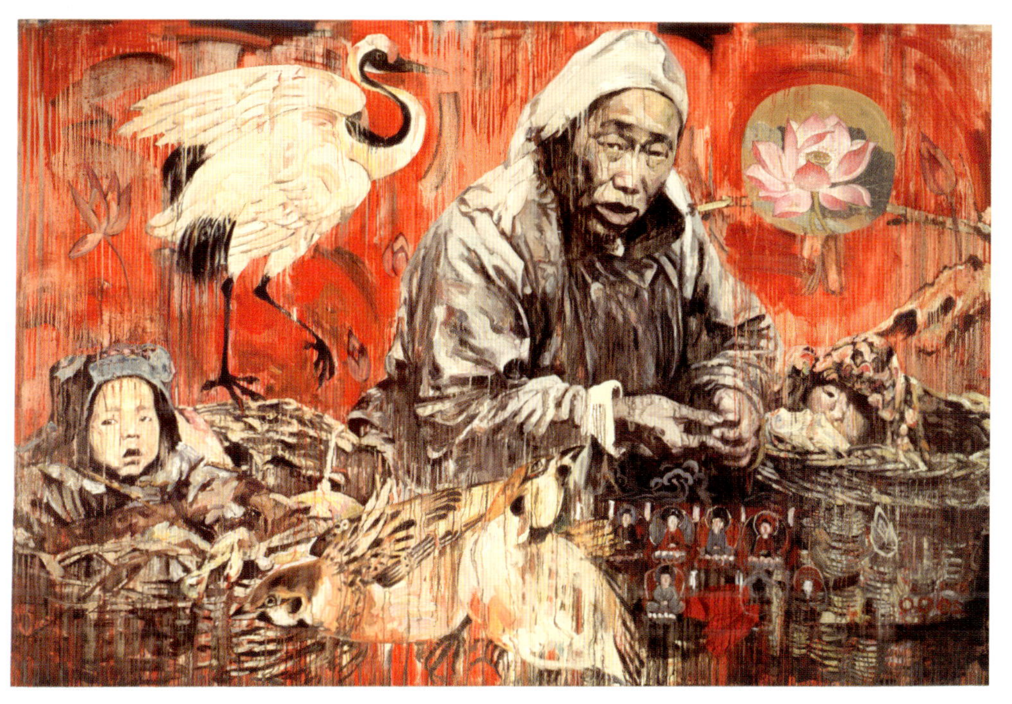

Refugees: Woman and Children | 2000
oil on canvas | 80 x 120 inches | Private collection

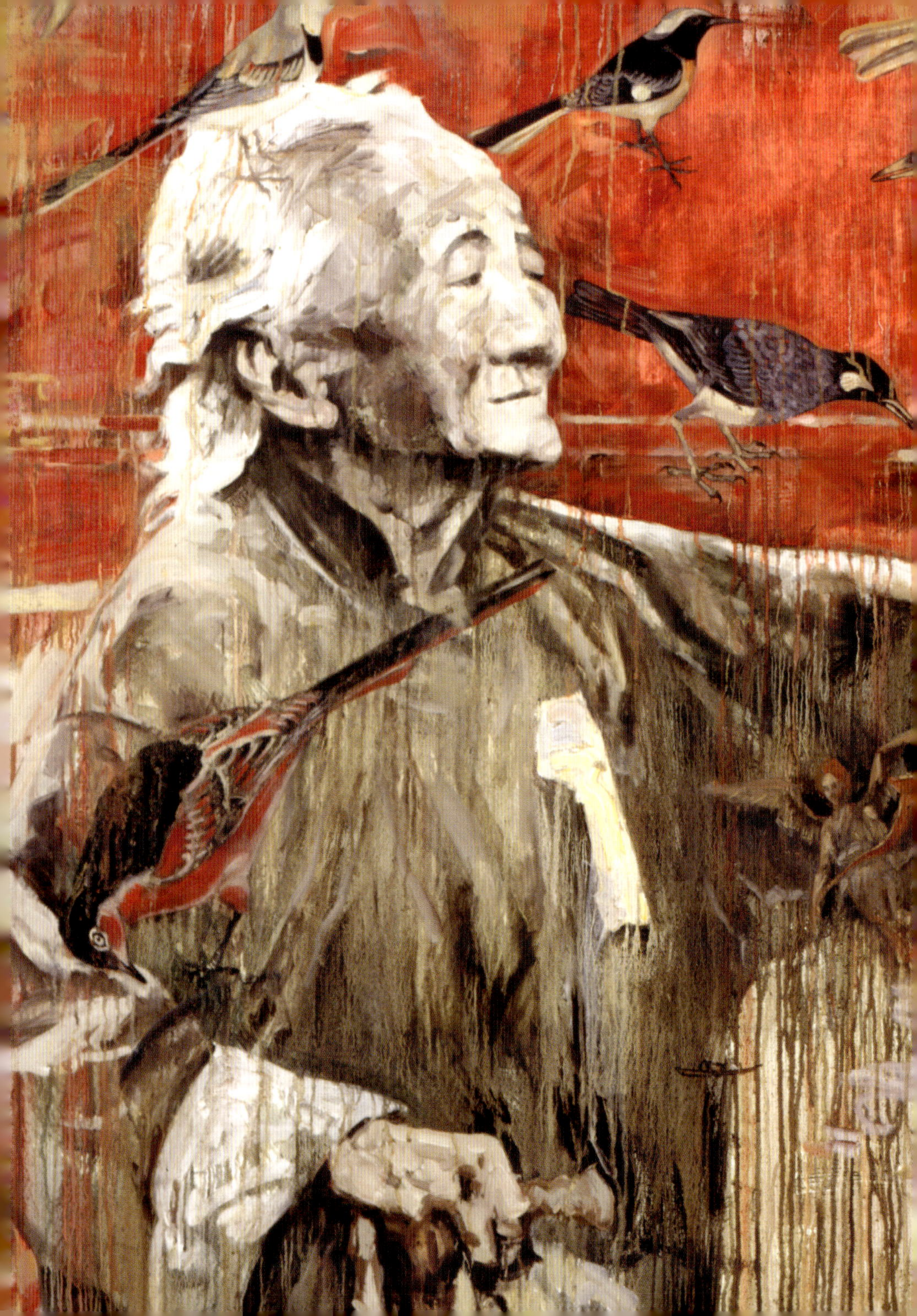

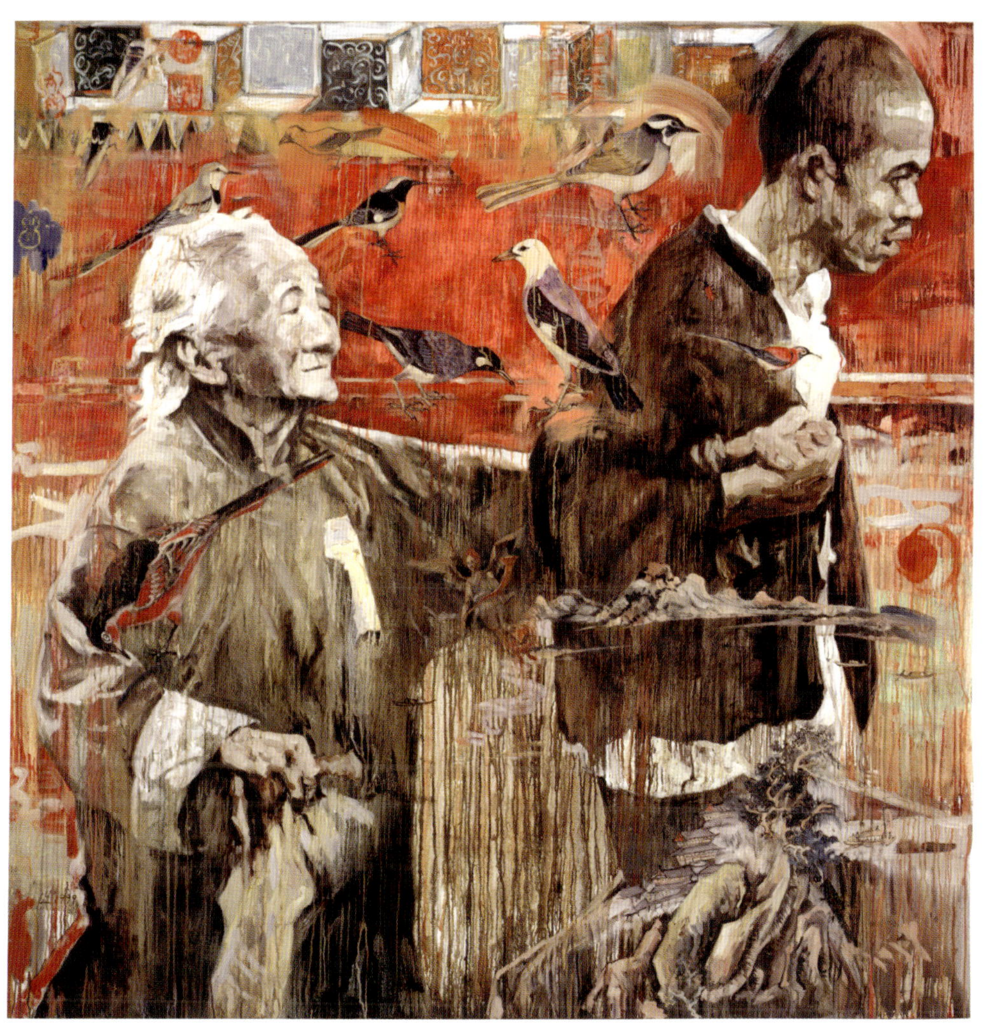

Refugees: Mother and Son | 1999
oil on canvas | 80 x 80 inches | Private collection

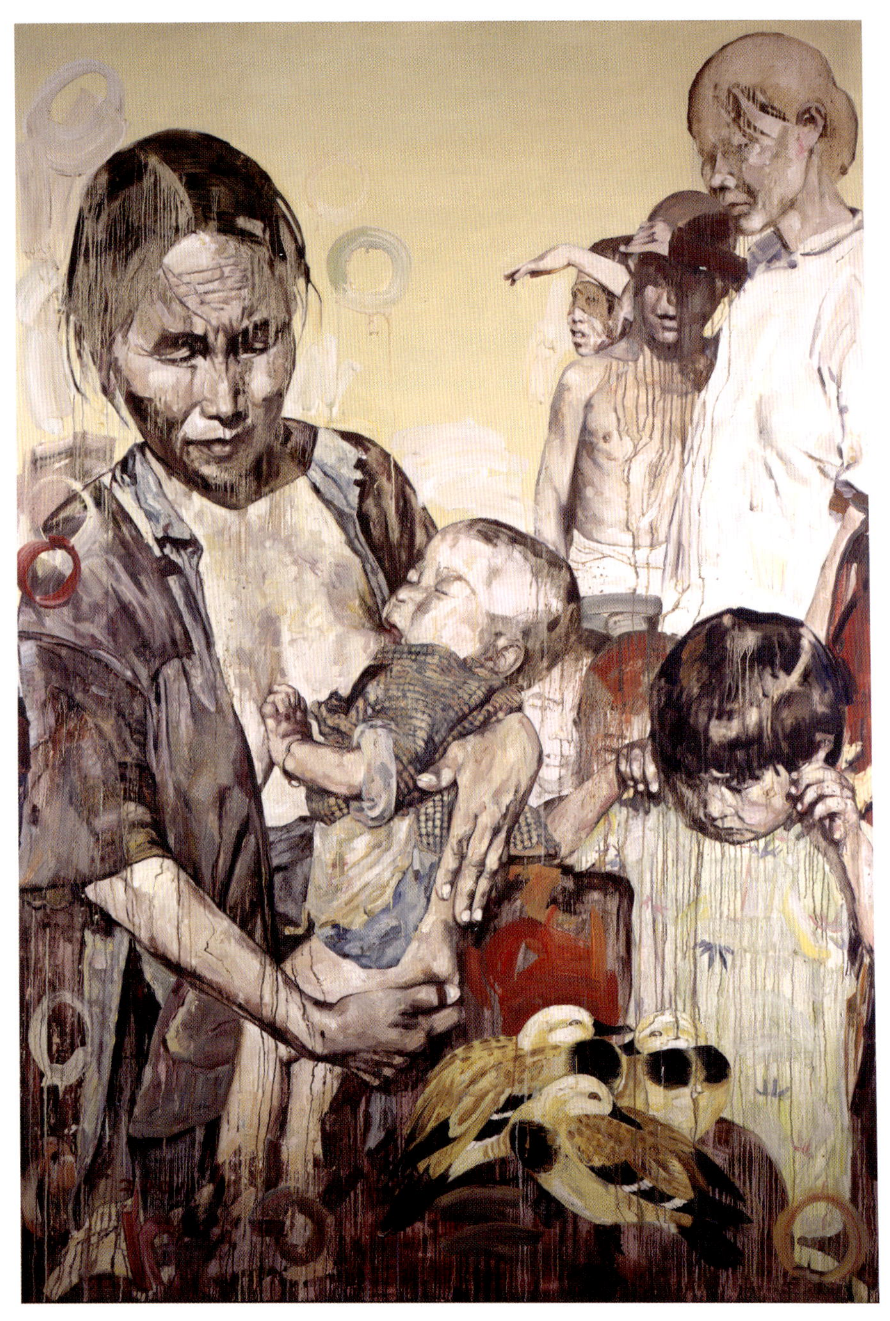

Refugee Opera | 2001
oil on canvas | 114 x 78 inches | Private collection

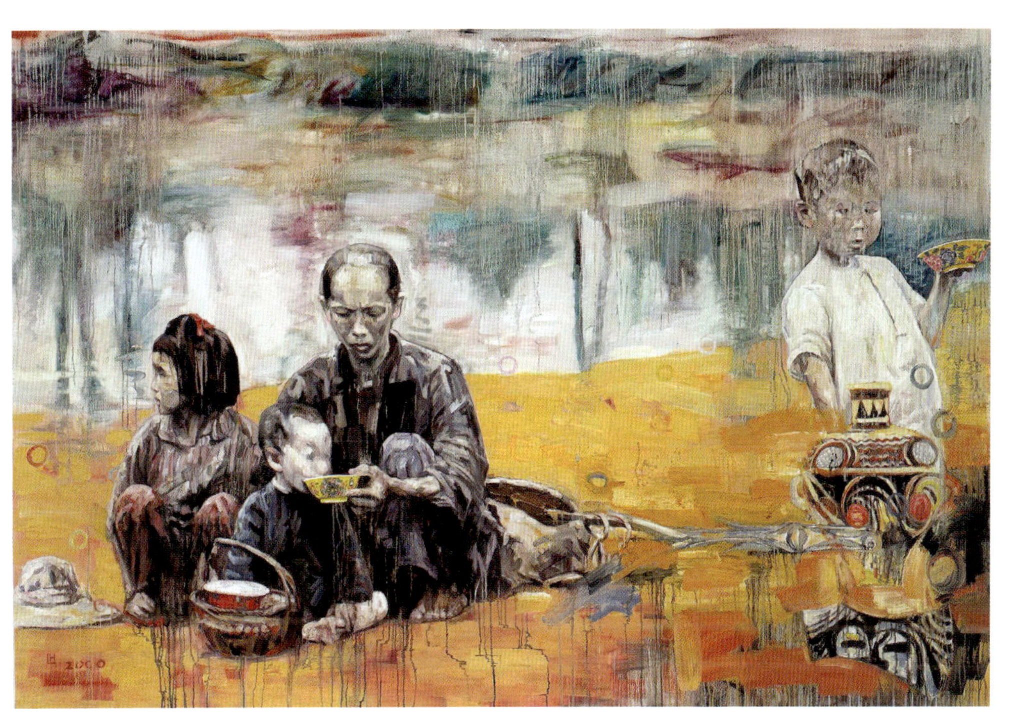

By the Rivers of Babylon | 2000
oil on canvas | 78 x 114 inches | Private collection

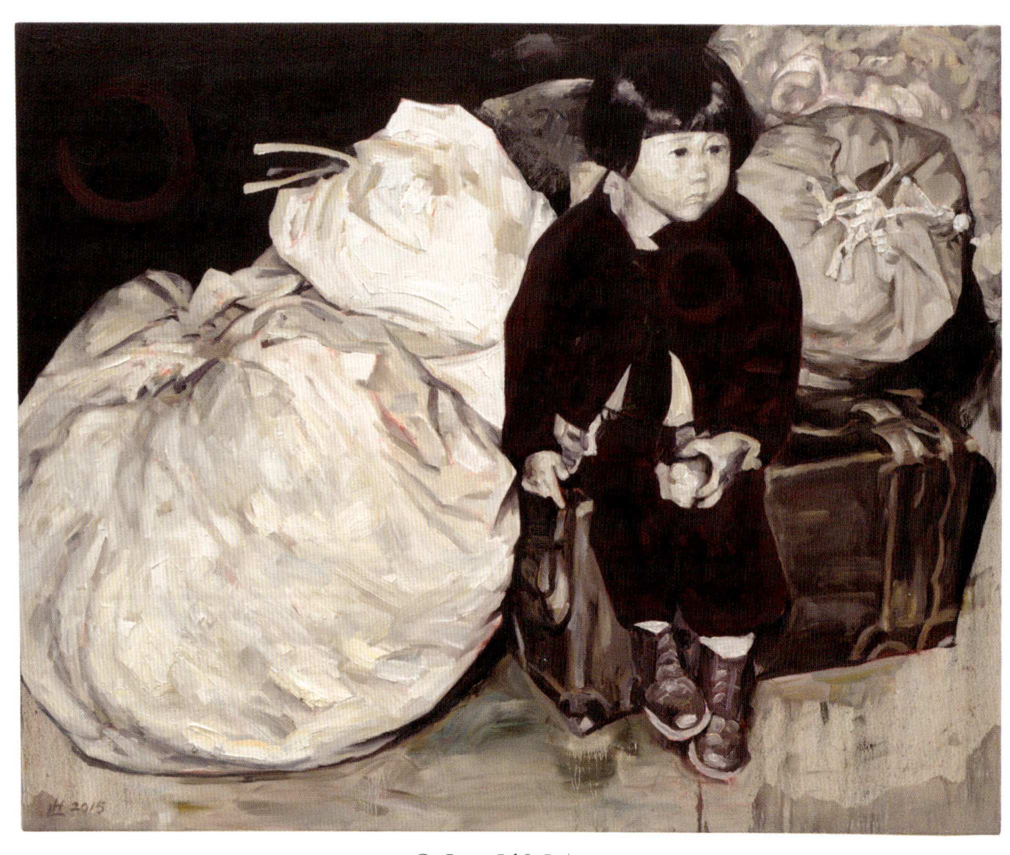

Oak and 10th | 2015
oil on canvas | 48 x 60 inches | Private collection

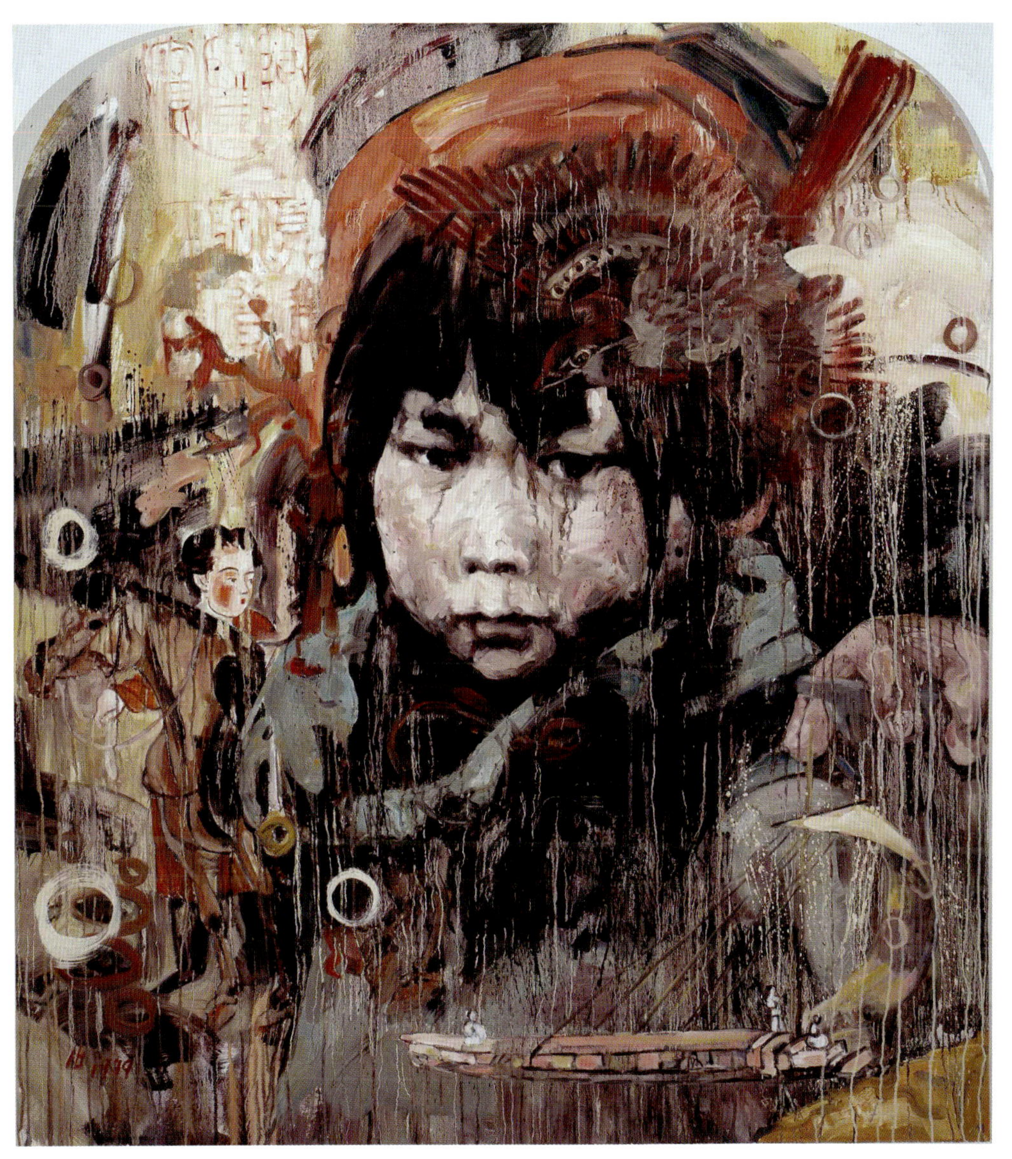

Refugees: Little Girl | 1999
oil on canvas | 68 x 60 inches | Private collection

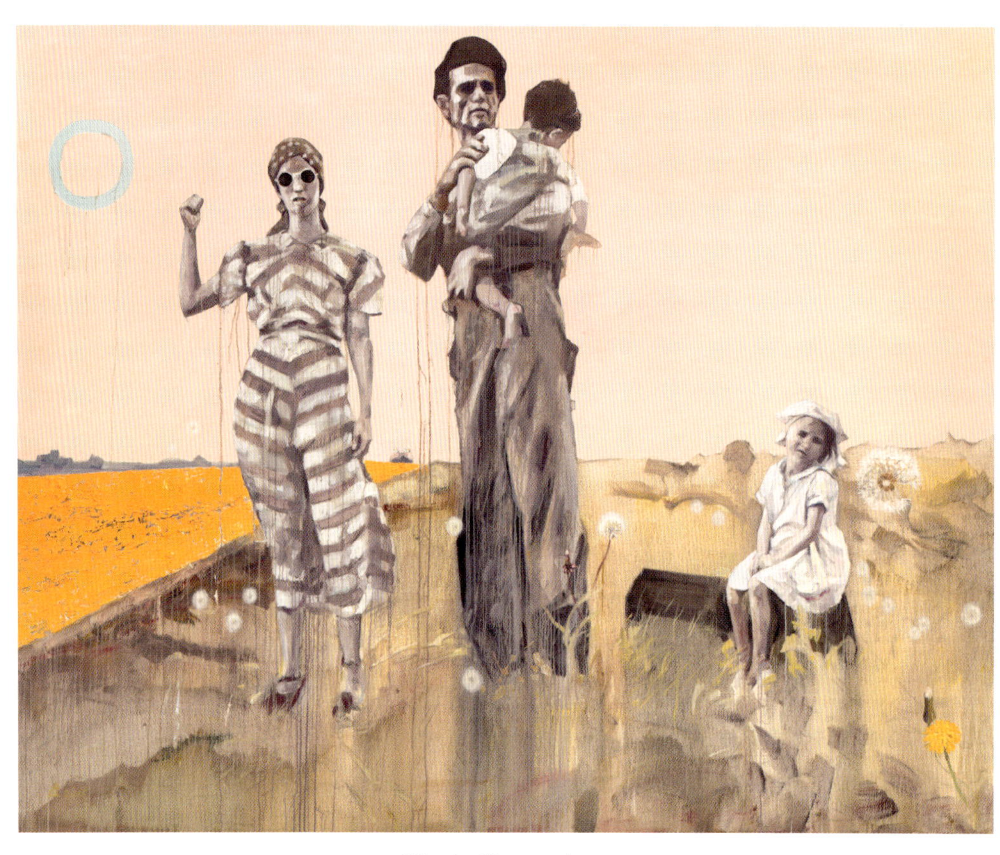

Not in Kansas | 2016

oil on canvas | 96 x 120 inches | University of Wyoming Art Museum

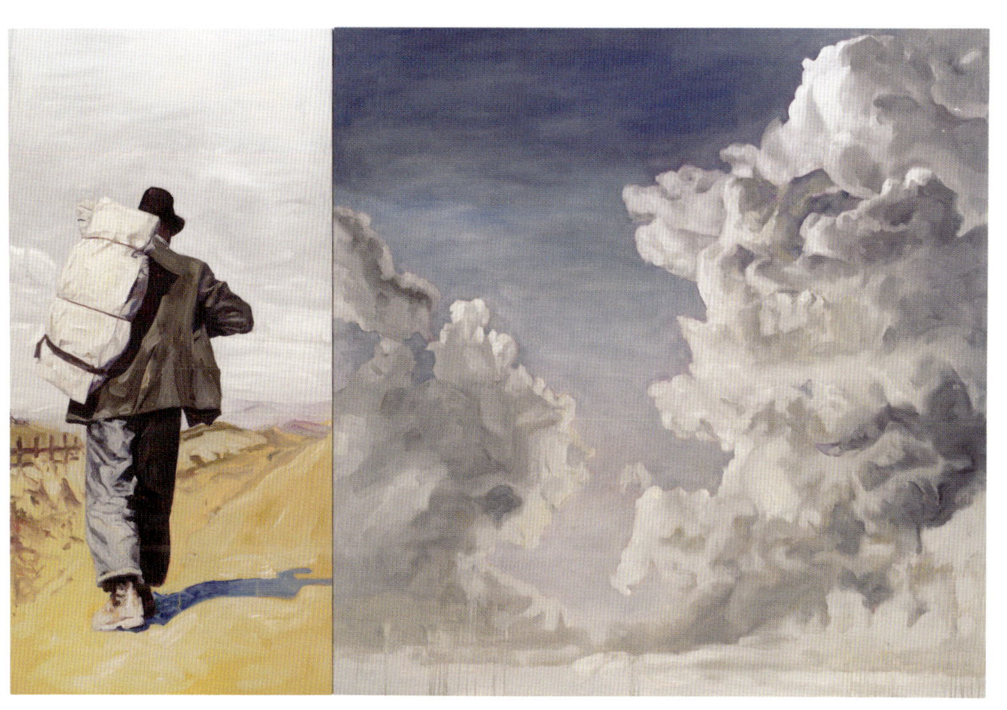

Bindlestiff | 2015

oil on canvas | 80 x 120 inches, diptych | Oakland Museum of California

Self-Portraits

Portraiture is one strand of my work, but I don't think of myself as a portraitist. I have never taken self-portraiture too seriously. Most of the paintings I've done of my likeness are ghosts of myself, or somehow lost, or beyond myself. They are not self-expressive or particularly self-reflective—they are usually just fleeting glimpses in an old photograph.

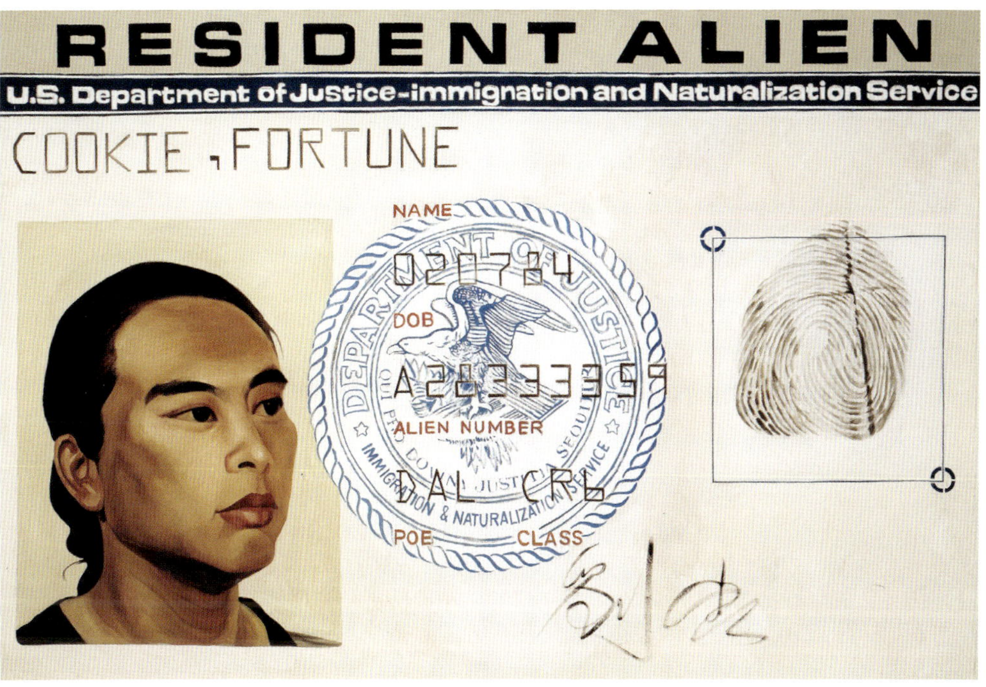

Resident Alien | 1988

oil on canvas | 60 x 90 inches | San José Museum of Art

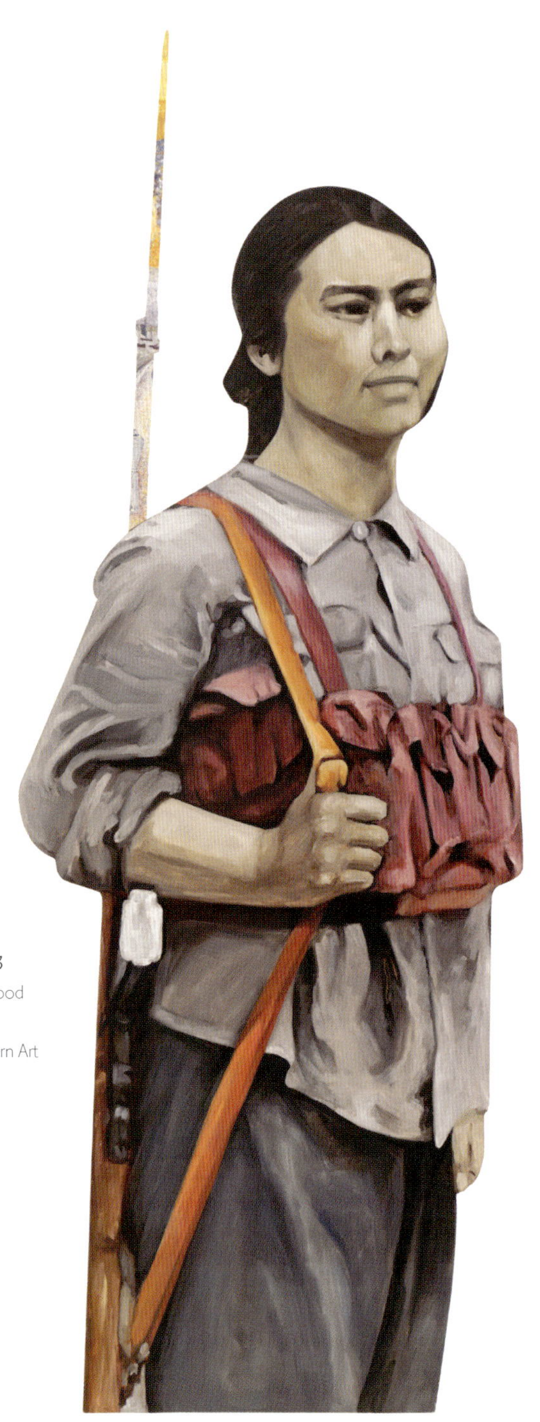

Avant-Garde | 1993
oil on shaped canvas, oil on wood
116 x 43 inches
San Francisco Museum of Modern Art

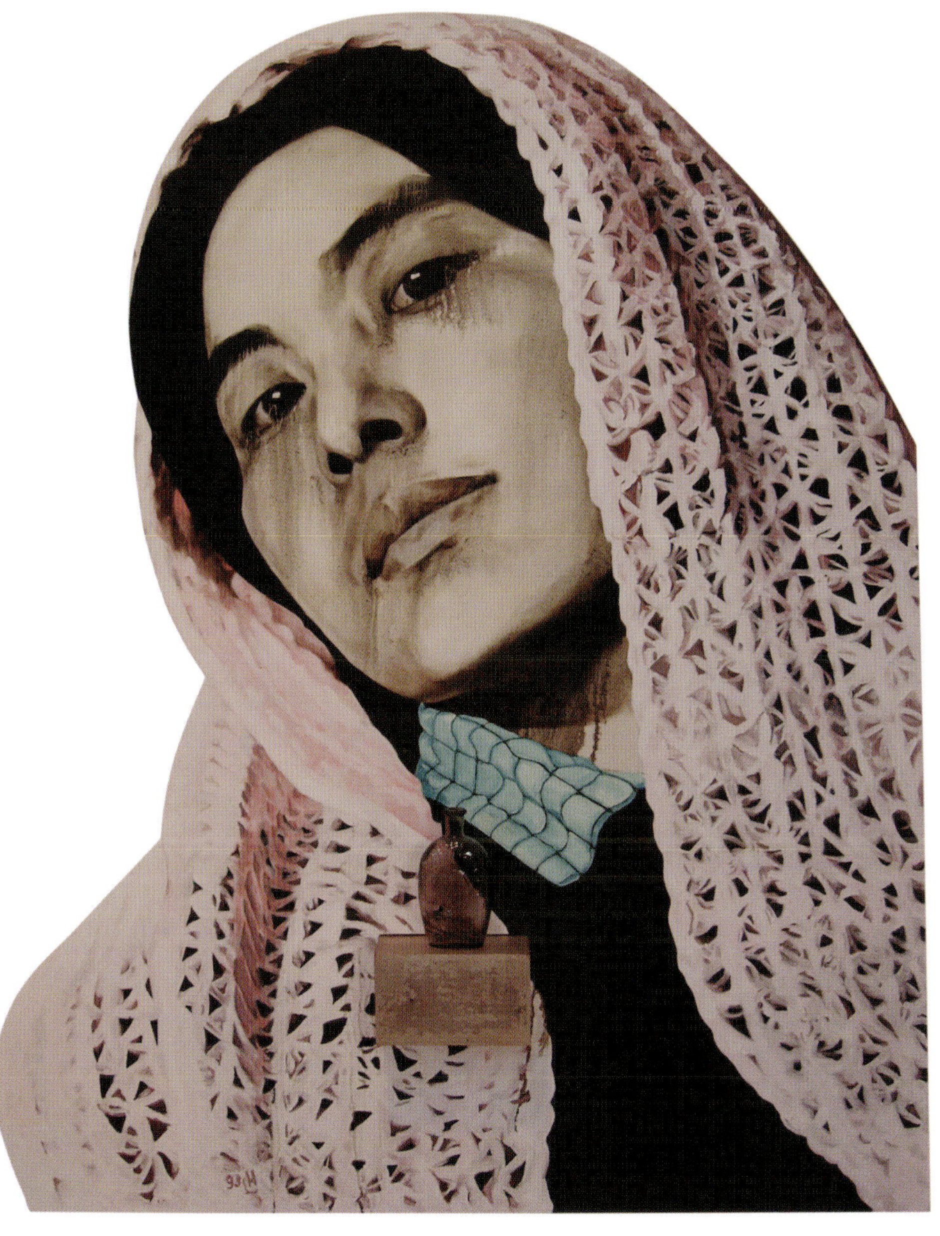

Daughter of the Revolution | 1993

oil on canvas, wood and antique glass bottle | 78.5 x 62 x 5.5 inches | Collection of the artist

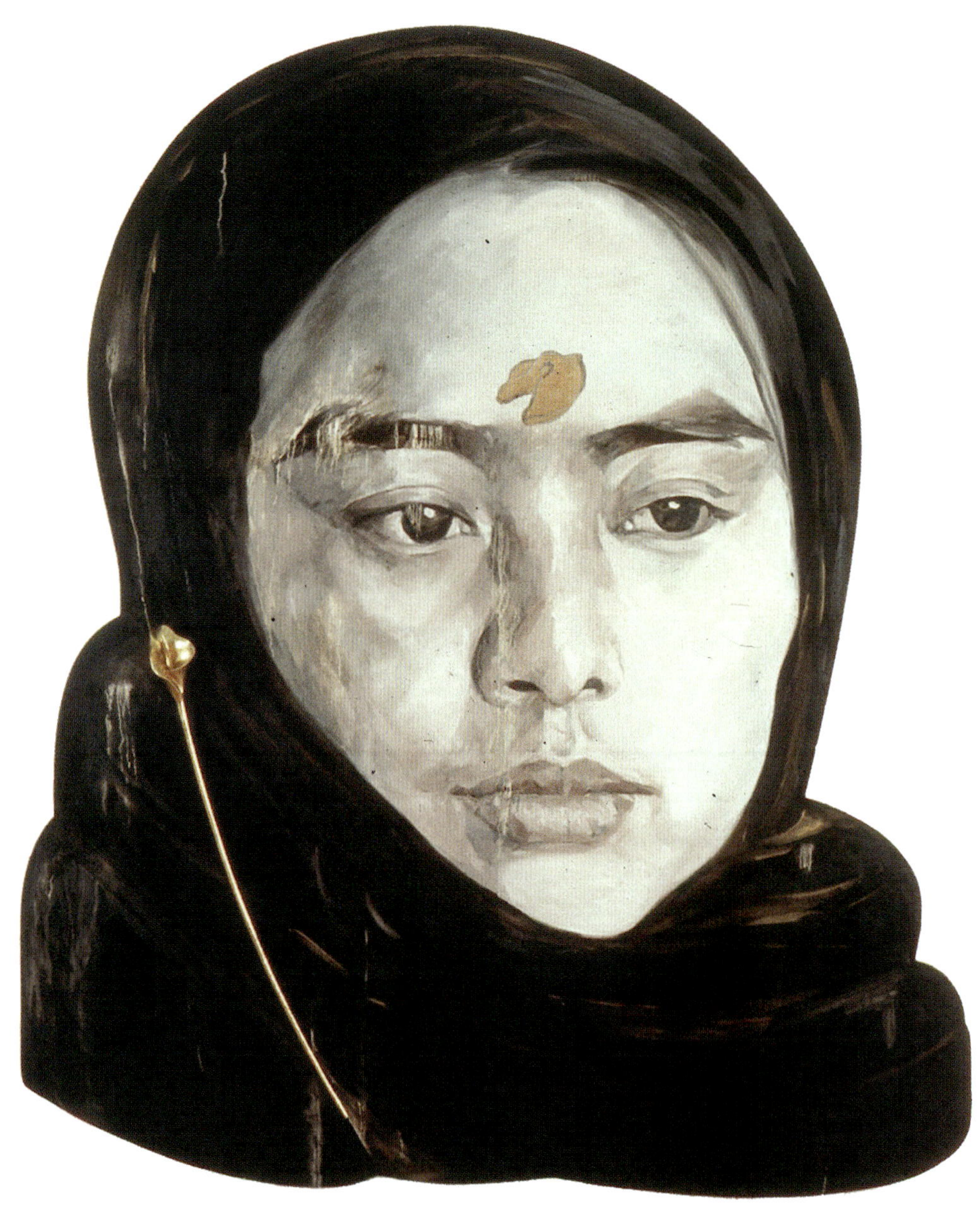

Golden Gate | 1994
oil on canvas, wood flower | 79 x 67 inches | Private collection

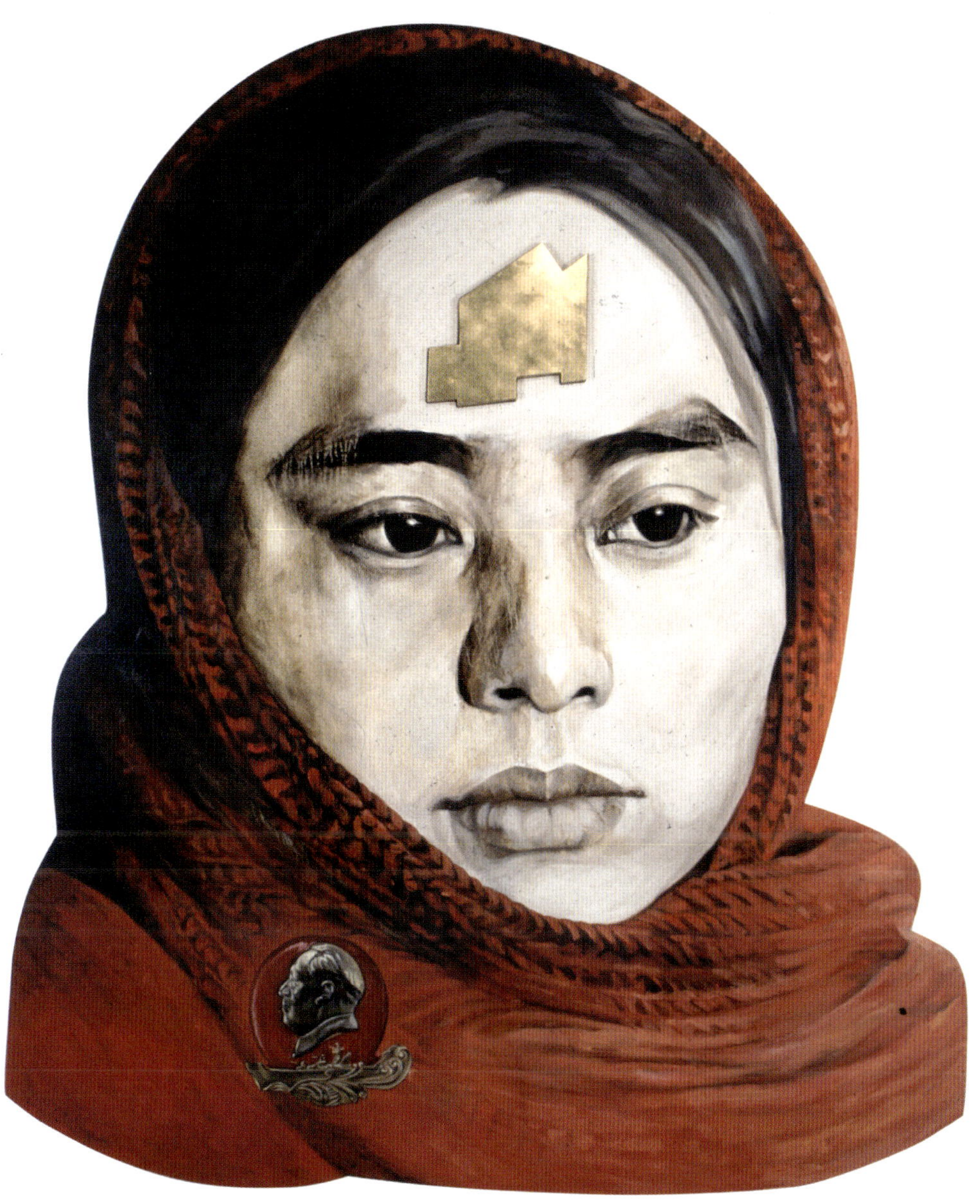

A Third World | 1994

oil on canvas, gold leaf on wood | 79 x 67 inches | Santa Barbara Museum of Art

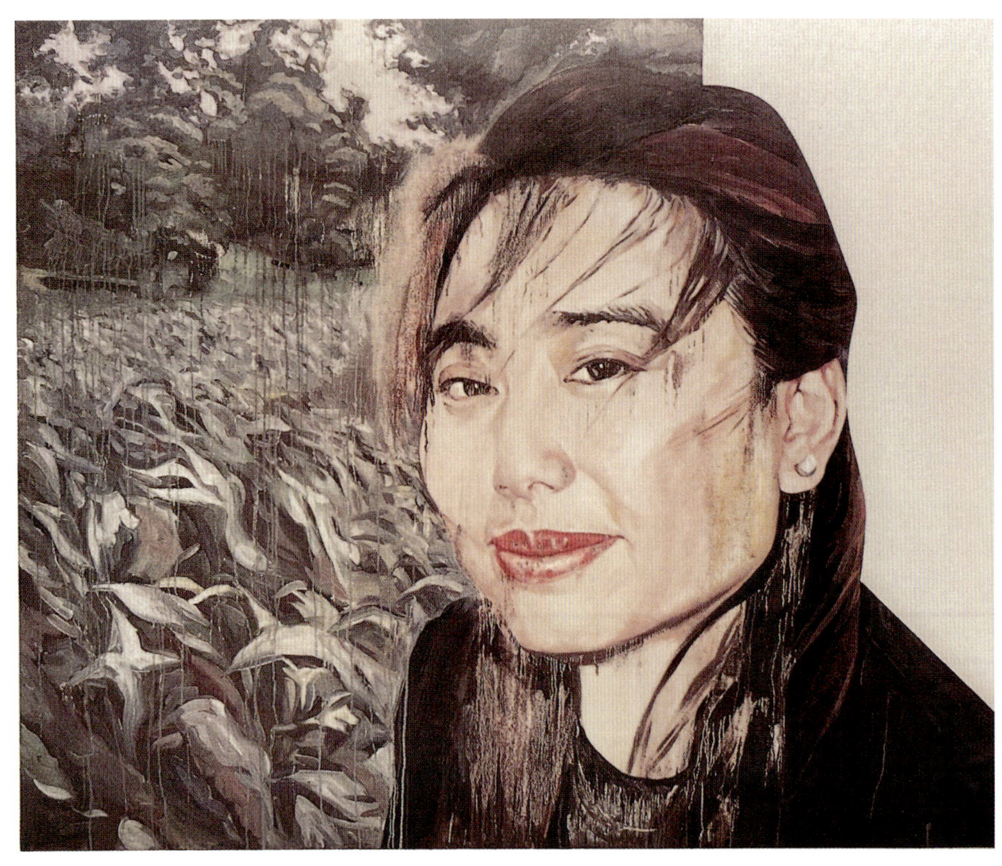

Burial at Little Golden Village | 1993
oil on canvas | 96 x 74 inches | Private collection

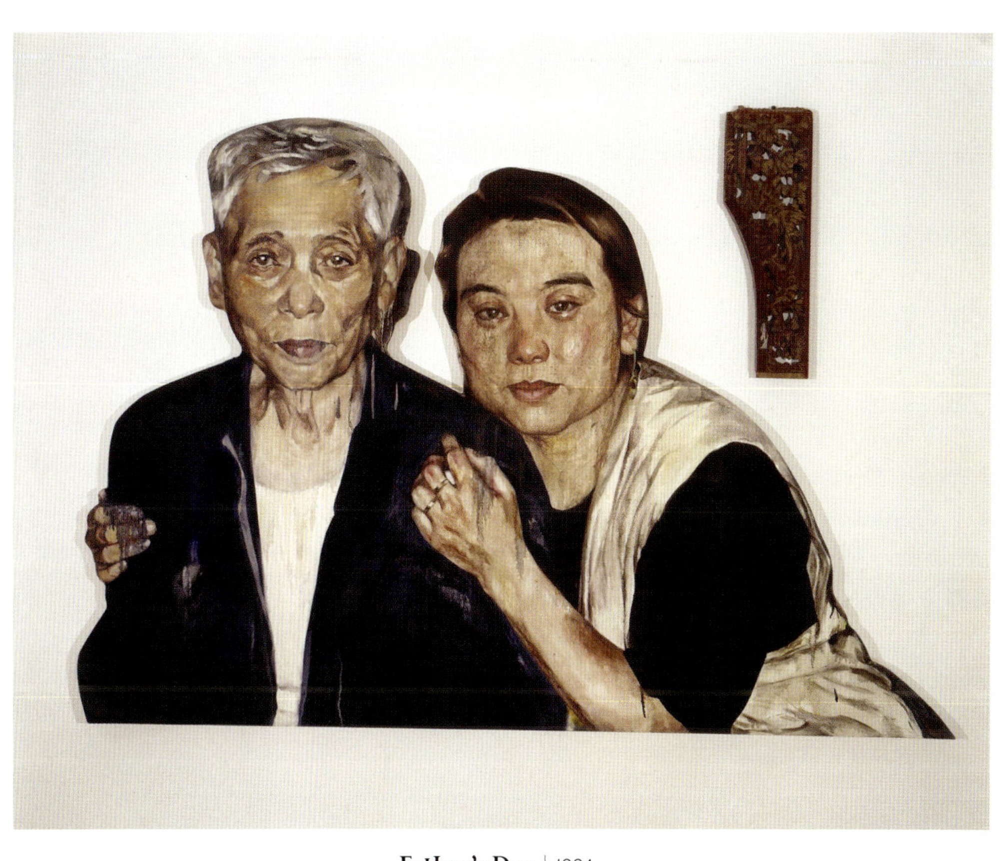

Father's Day | 1994
oil on canvas, architectural panel | 54 x 72 inches | Private collection

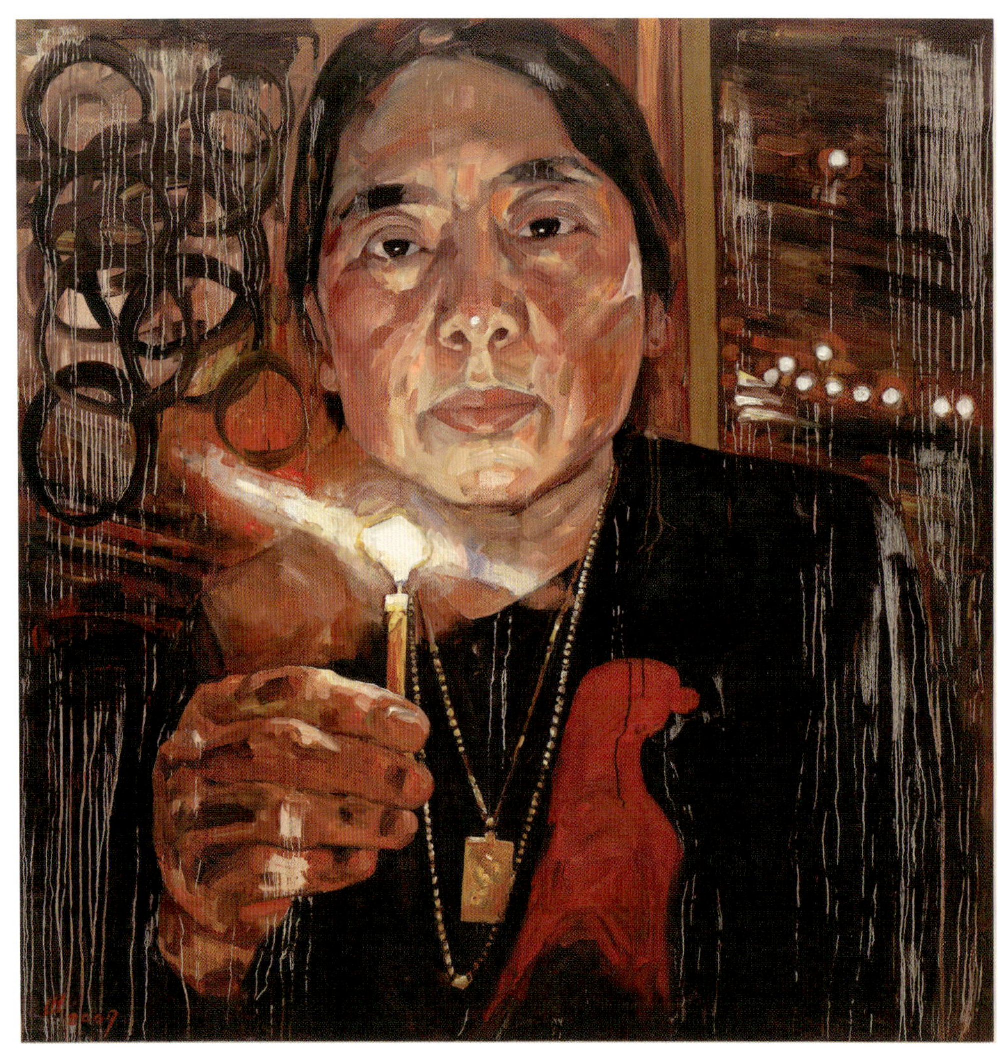

Candle | 2009
oil on canvas | 72 x 72 inches | Private collection

Year of the Rat

In 2008 I turned sixty. According to the Chinese ancient way of counting, the sixtieth year is a cycle, a *Jiaze*. Now, since 2020 is a rat year and the beginning of a new sixty-year cycle, I intend to make another self-portrait. I'll use the same diptych format as the finished rat year portraits—one side is a painting of me from that year (1948, 1960, 1972, 1984, 1996, and 2008), while the other panel is an image of a drawing I did in the same year. I consider all of the rat year portraits as ghosts of myself. When you finish each one it becomes past tense. If I'm around for the next rat year in 2032 I hope I can make another one.

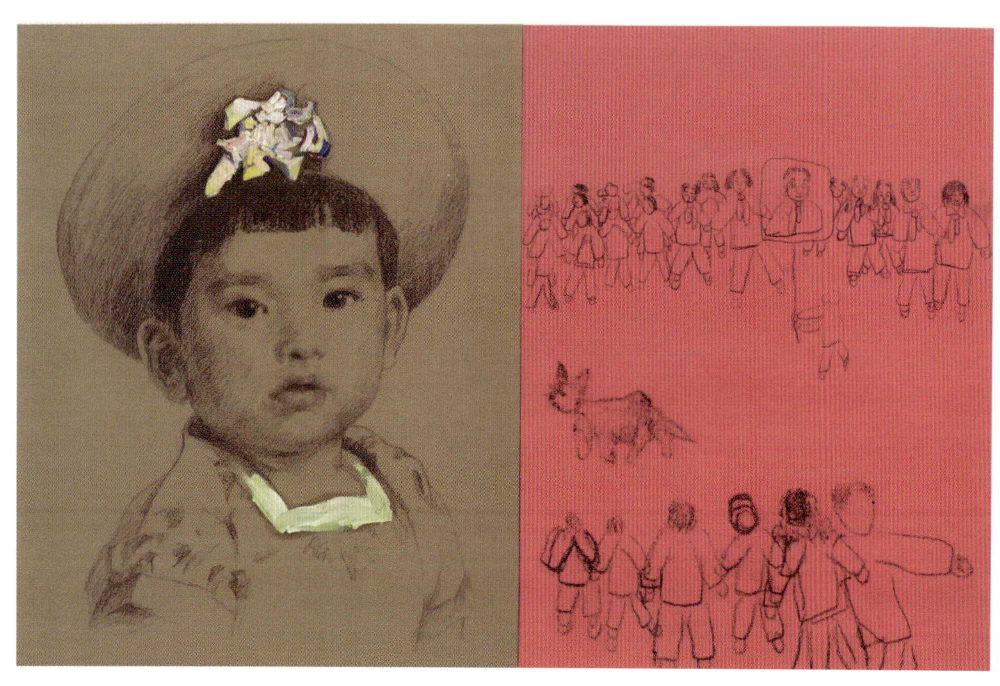

Rat Year 1948 | 2008

oil on linen and mixed media on wood panel | 64 x 100 inches | Collection of the artist

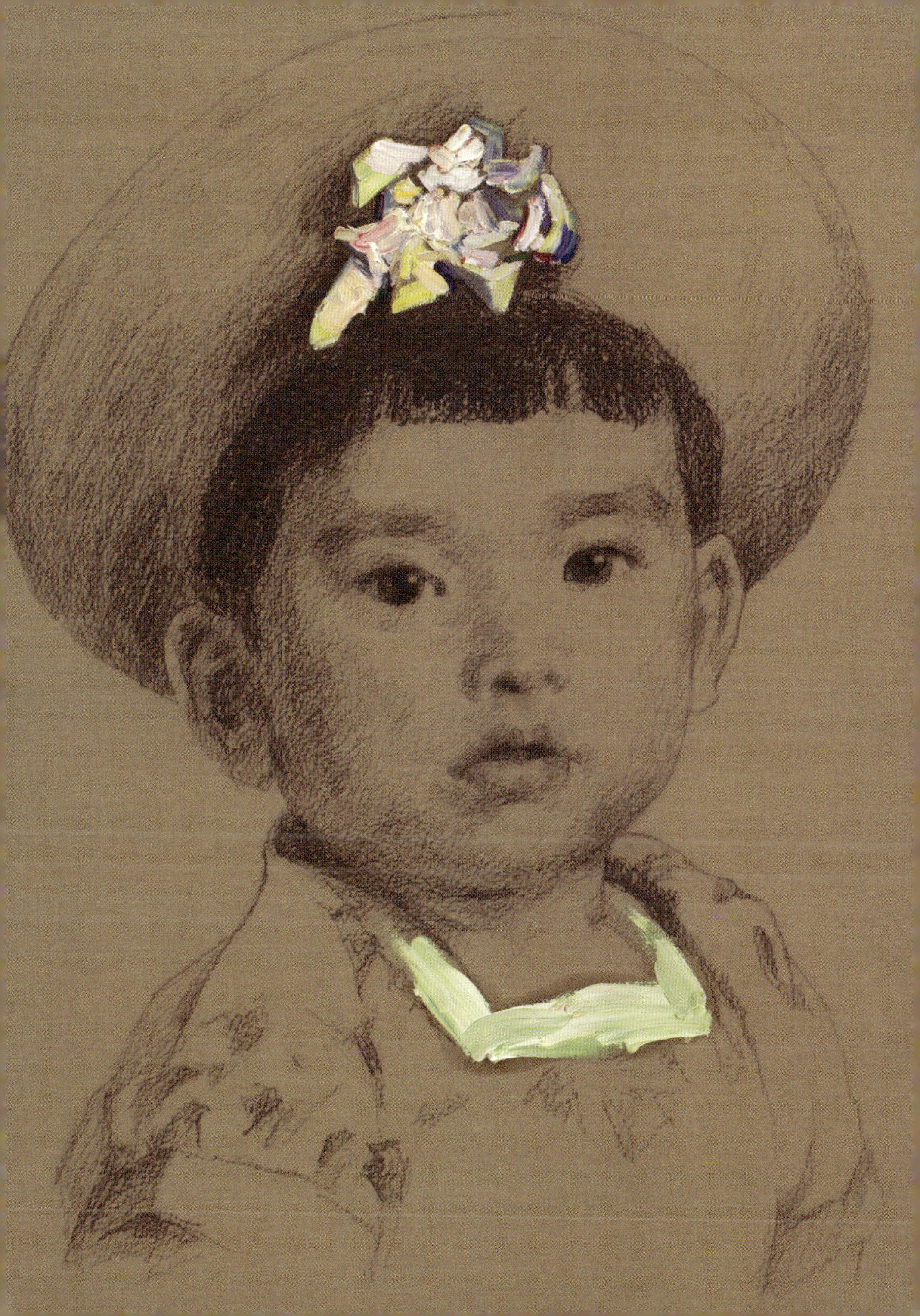

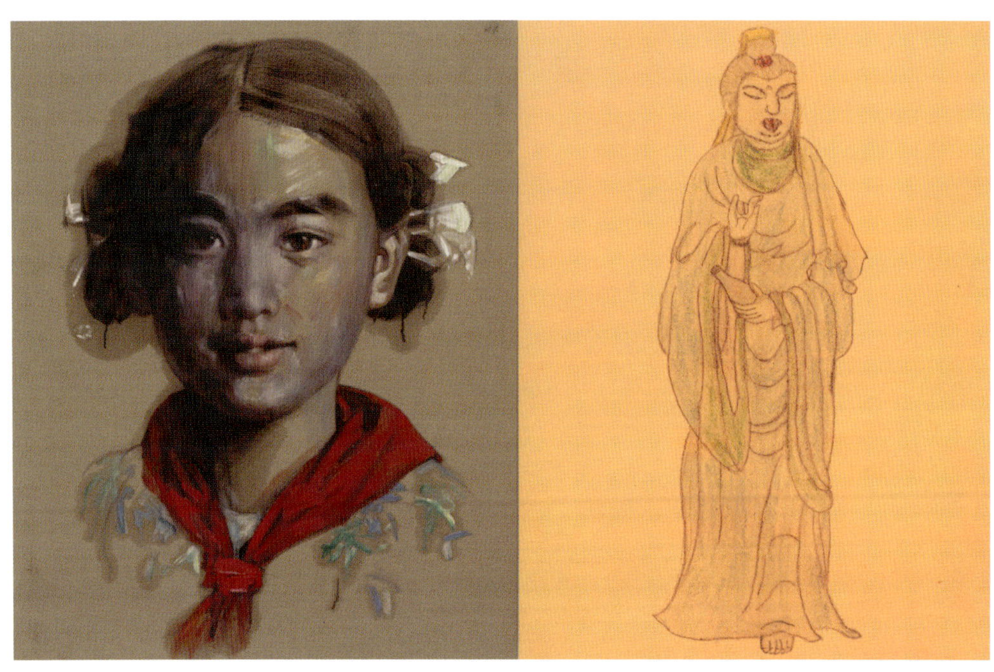

Rat Year 1960 | 2008

oil on linen and mixed media on wood panel | 64 x 100 inches | Collection of the artist

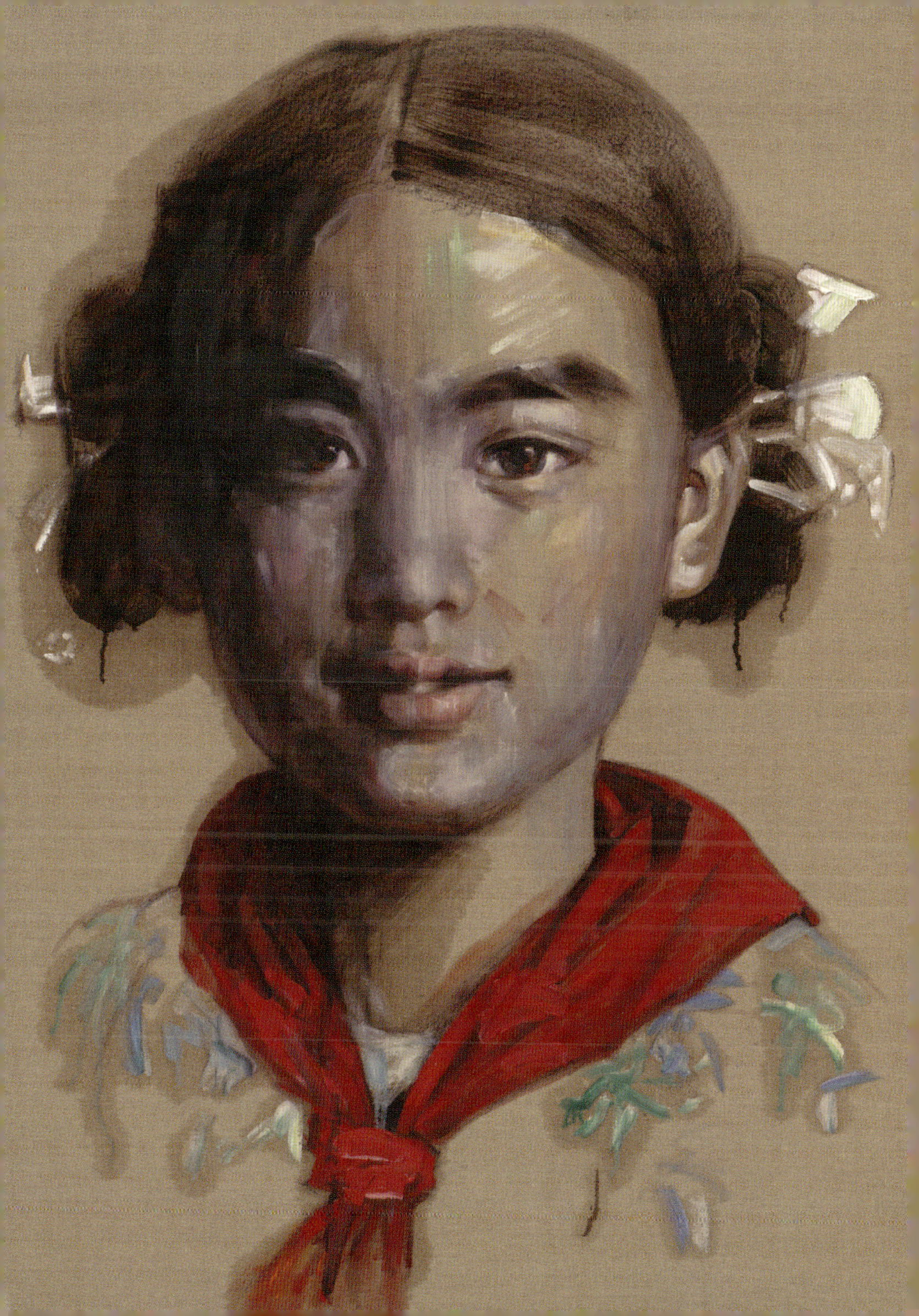

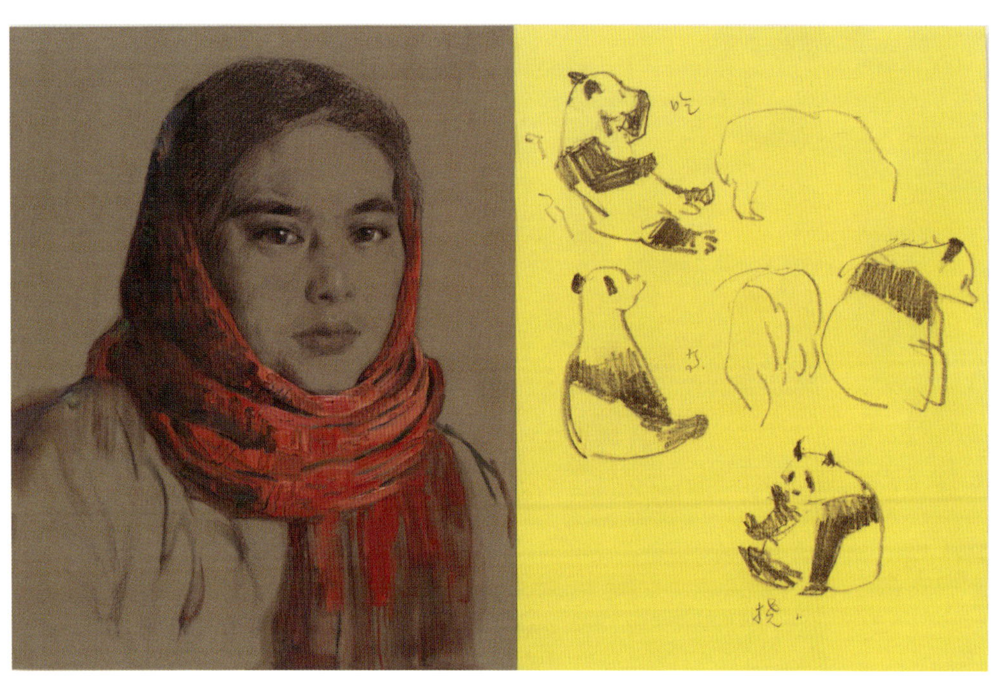

Rat Year 1972 | 2008

oil on linen and mixed media on wood panel | 64 x 100 inches | Collection of the artist

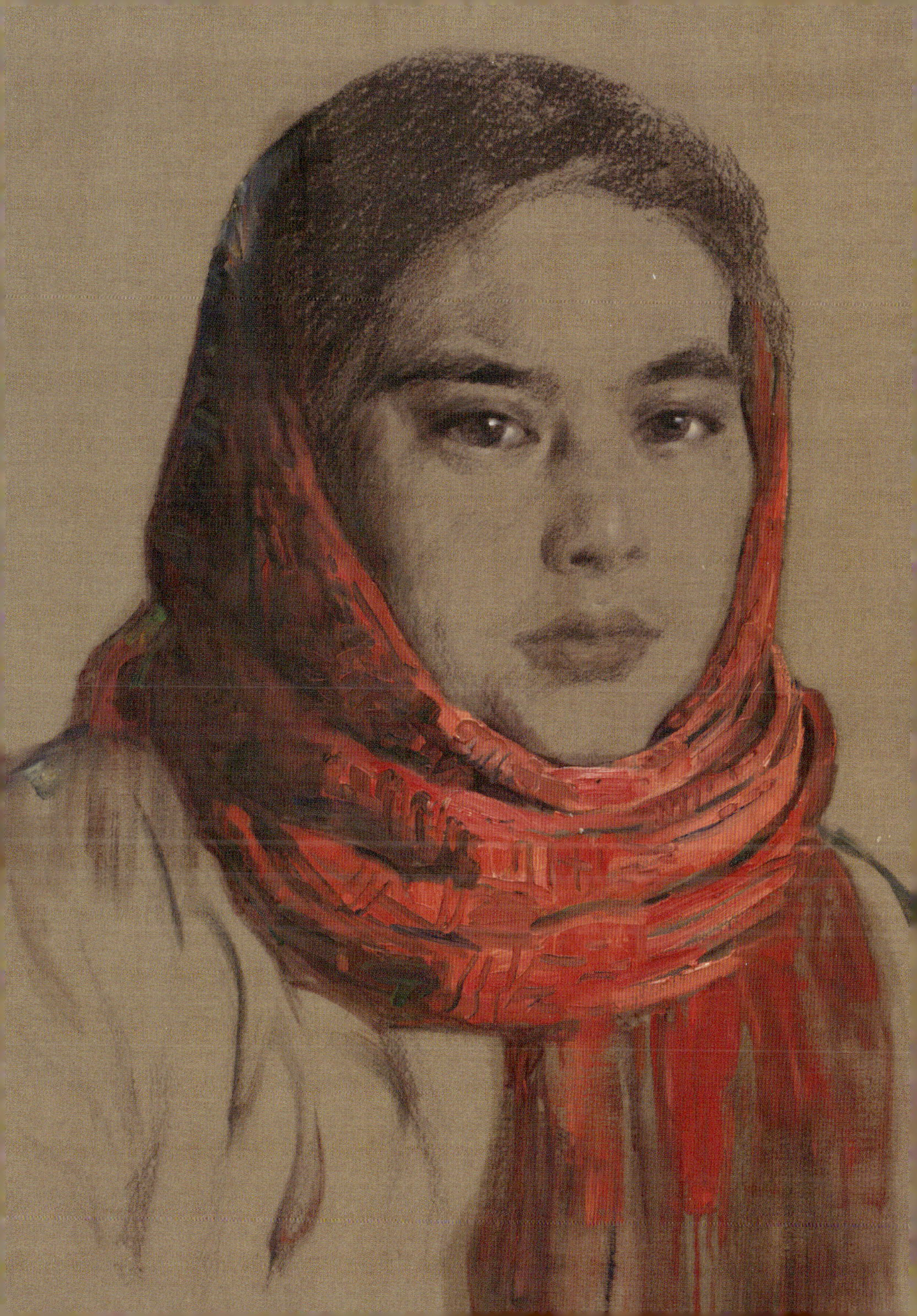

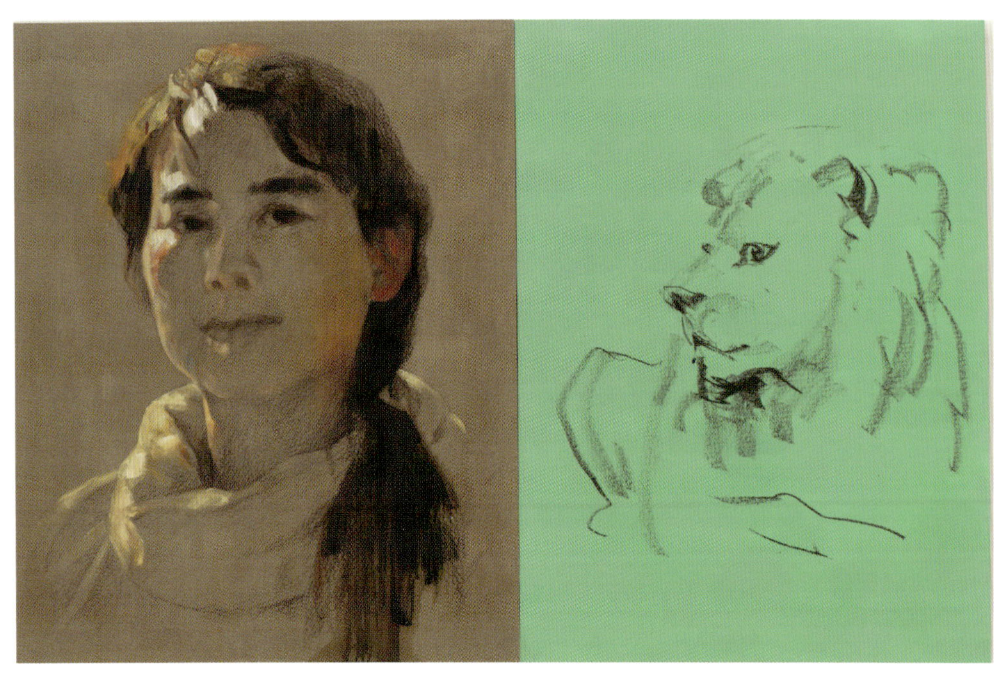

Rat Year 1984 | 2008

oil on linen and mixed media on wood panel | 64 x 100 inches | Collection of the artist

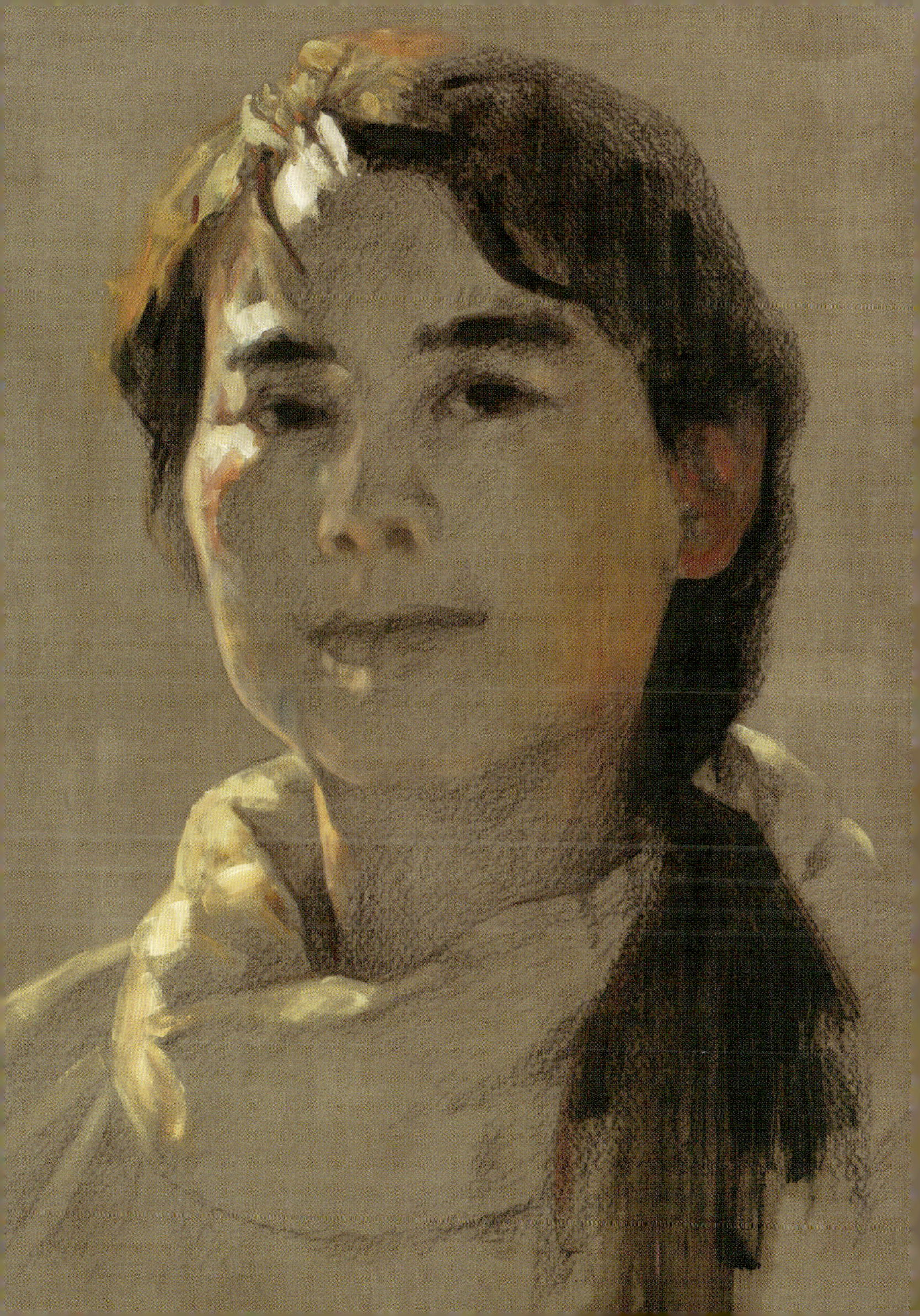

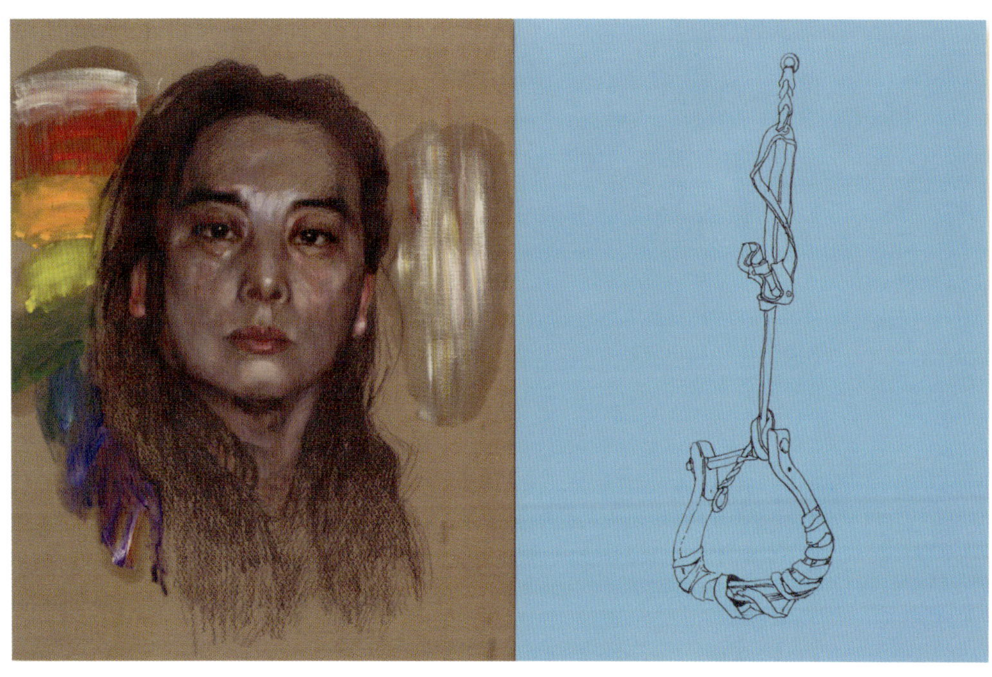

Rat Year 1996 | 2008

oil on linen and mixed media on wood panel | 64 x 100 inches | Collection of the artist

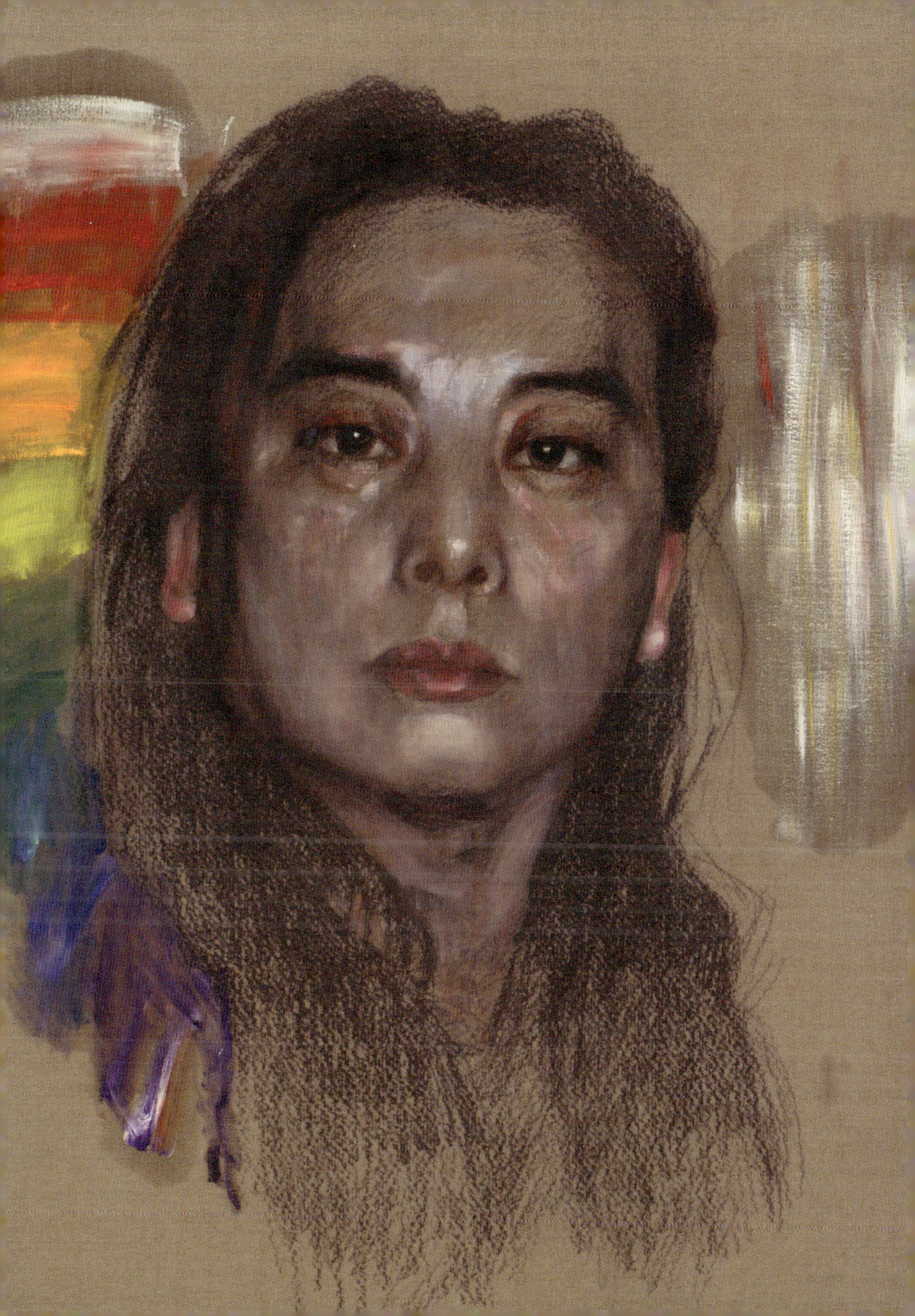

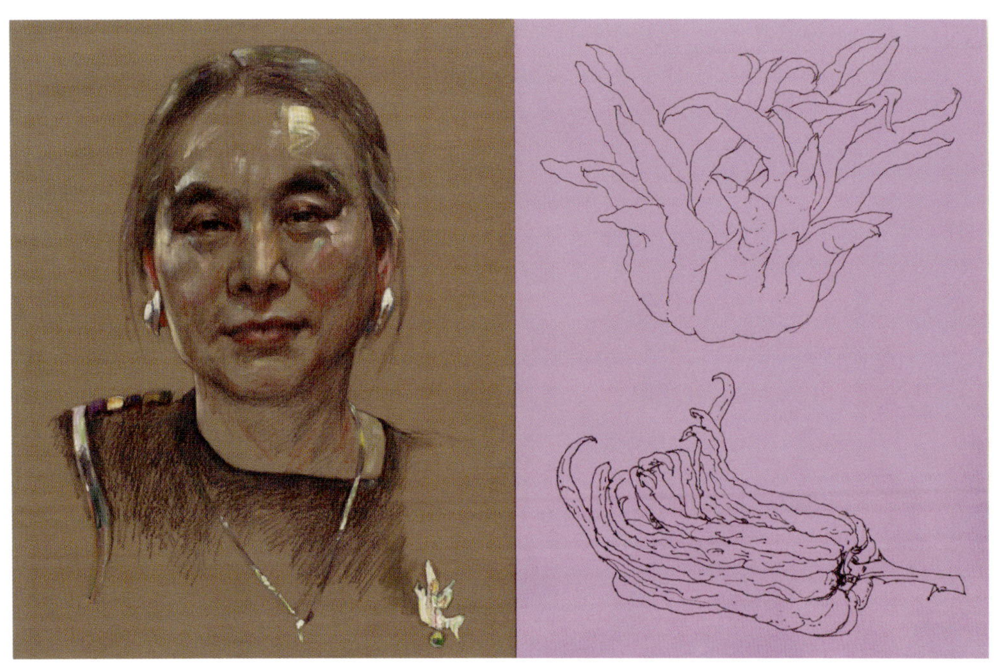

Rat Year 2008 | 2008

oil on linen and mixed media on wood panel | 64 x 100 inches | Collection of the artist

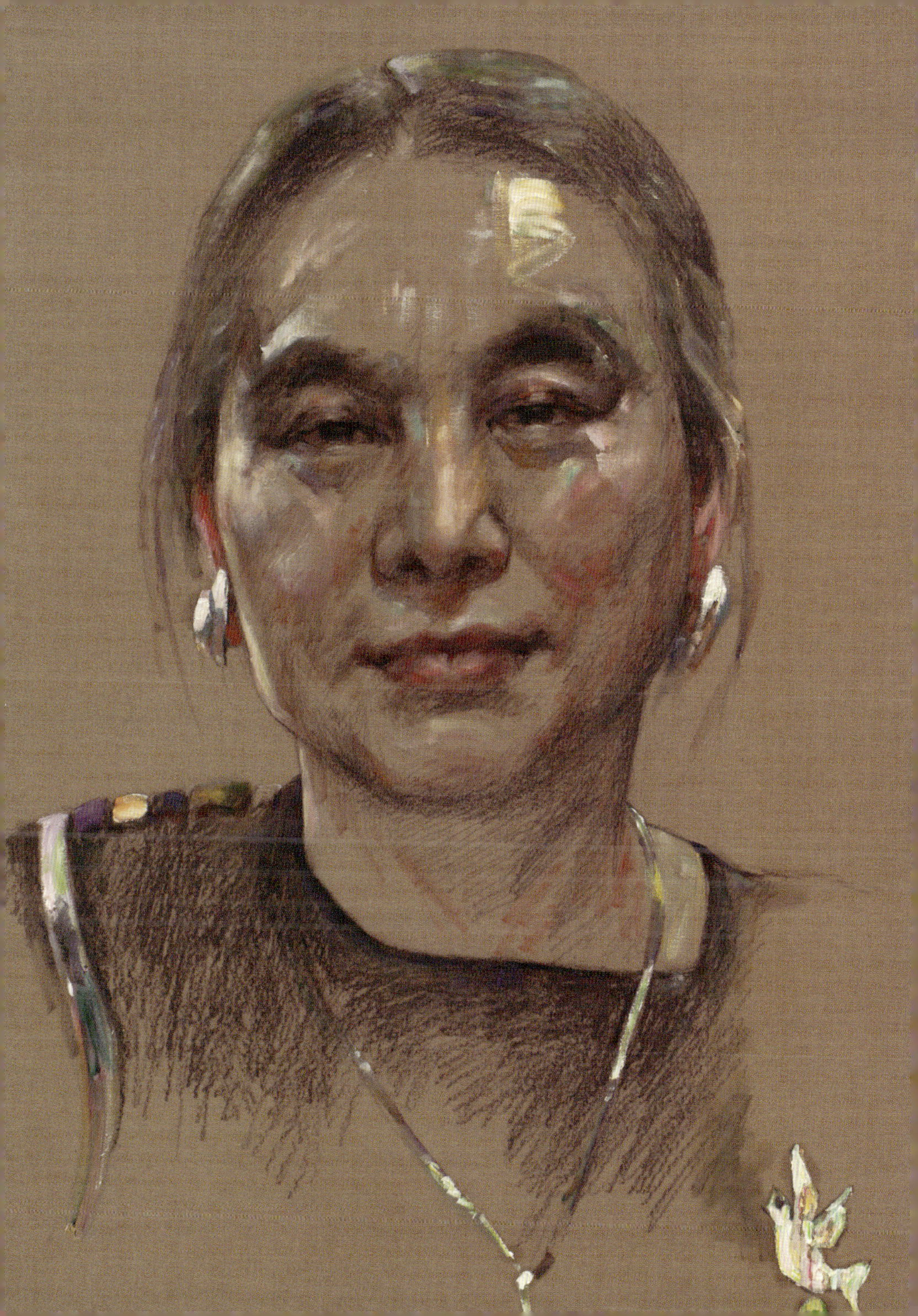

Hung Liu

Hung Liu was born in Changchun, China, in 1948, growing up during the Maoist regime. Initially trained in the Socialist Realist style, Liu studied mural painting as a graduate student at the Central Academy of Fine Art in Beijing, before immigrating to the US in 1984 to attend the University of California, San Diego, where she studied under Allan Kaprow, the American originator of Happenings, as well as Moira Roth, an influential feminist art historian.

Known for paintings based on historical Chinese photographs, Liu's subjects over the years have been prostitutes, refugees, street performers, soldiers, laborers, and prisoners, among others. As a painter, Liu challenges the documentary authority of historical photographs by subjecting them to the more reflective process of painting. Much of the meaning of Liu's painting comes from the way the washes and drips dissolve the documentary images, suggesting the passage of memory into history, while working to uncover the cultural and personal narratives fixed—but often concealed— in the photographic instant. Washing her subjects in veils of dripping linseed oil, she both preserves and destroys the image. Liu has invented a kind of weeping realism that surrenders to the erosion of memory and the passage of time, while also bringing faded photographic images vividly to life as rich, facile paintings. She summons the ghosts of history to the present. In effect, Liu turns old photographs into new paintings.

Recently, Liu has shifted her focus from Chinese to American subjects. By training her attention on the displaced individuals and wandering families of the American Dustbowl, Liu finds a landscape of migration, struggle, and humanity that for her is familiar terrain, having been raised in China during an era of epic revolution, tumult, and displacement. The 1930s Oakies and bindlestiffs wandering like ghosts through Liu's new paintings are American peasants, many on their way to California, the promised land. For her Dorothea Lange–inspired works, Liu has developed a kind of topographic painting technique in which she maps an image with colored lines, the richness of which belies the real-world poverty of her subjects. She then paints within and between those lines until the overall image emerges. In this way, the new paintings are closely woven to Lange's photographs while also releasing the energy of color like a radiant of hope from beneath the gray tones of history.

A two-time recipient of a National Endowment for the Arts Fellowship in painting, Liu also received a Lifetime Achievement Award in Printmaking from the Southern Graphics Council International in 2011. A retrospective of Liu's work, "Summoning Ghosts: The Art and Life of Hung Liu," was recently organized by the Oakland Museum of California, and toured nationally through 2015. In a review of that show, the *Wall Street Journal* called Liu "the greatest Chinese painter in the US." Liu's works have been exhibited extensively and collected by the San Francisco Museum of Modern Art, the Whitney Museum of American Art, New York, the Nelson-Atkins Museum and the Kemper Museum, Kansas City, the National Gallery of Art, Washington, DC, the Asian Art Museum and the de Young Museum of San Francisco, and the Los Angeles County Museum, among others. Liu's portrait-based paintings are the focus of a 2021 retrospective at the National Portrait Gallery, Smithsonian Institution, Washington, DC. Liu currently lives in Oakland, California. She is Professor Emerita at Mills College, where she taught from 1990.

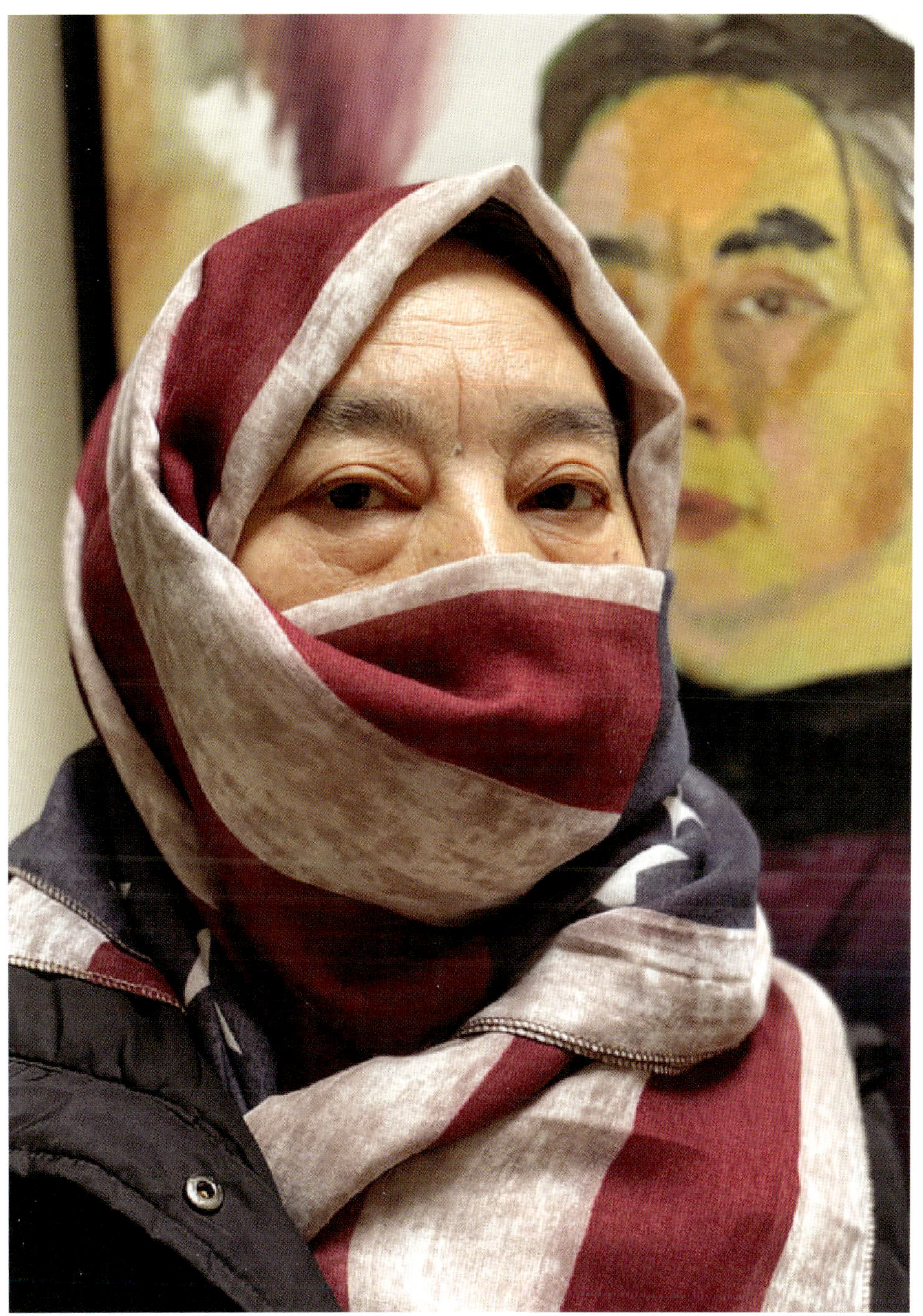

COLOPHON

Published by Kelly's Cove Press
October 2020

Typeface
Prior Sans and Prior Serif

Printing and Binding
Versa Press Inc.
East Peoria, Illinois

Art
Hung Liu

Cover and interior design
Lynn Phelps

RICHARD DIEBENKORN

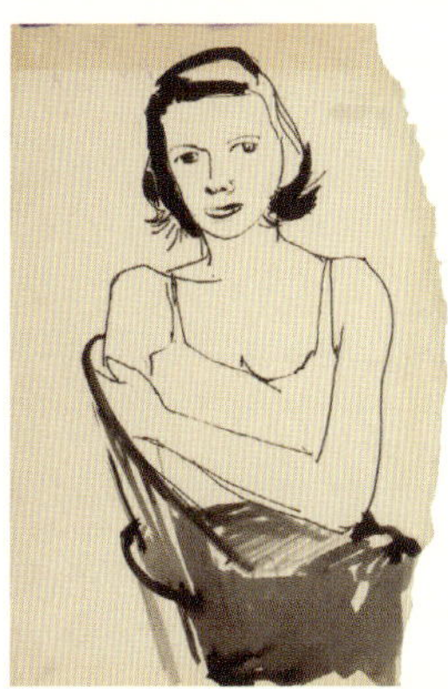

FROM THE MODEL

RICHARD DIEBENKORN

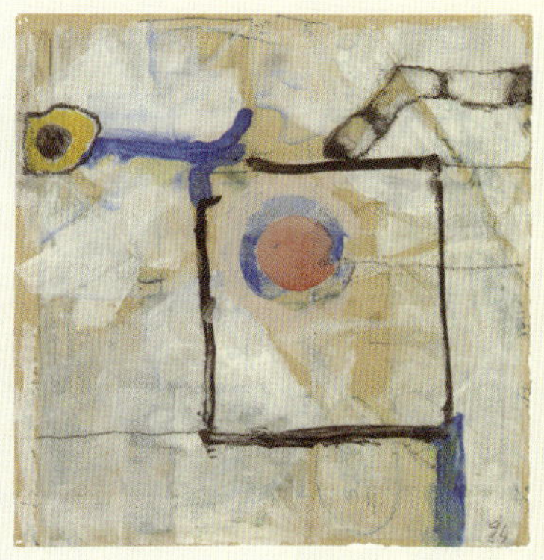

ABSTRACTIONS ON PAPER

RICHARD DIEBENKORN

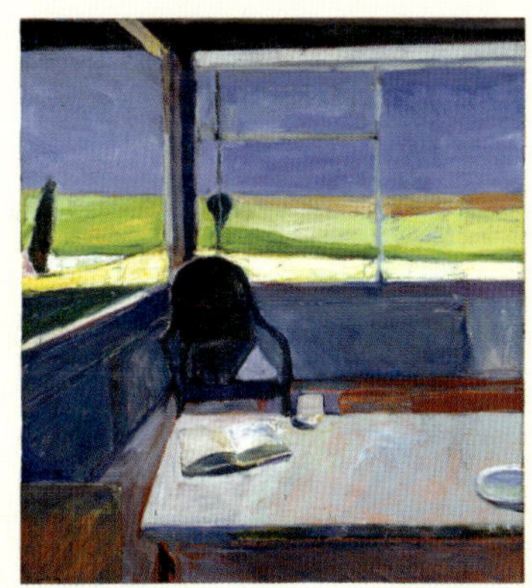

STILL LIFES AND LANDSCAPES

RICHARD DIEBENKORN

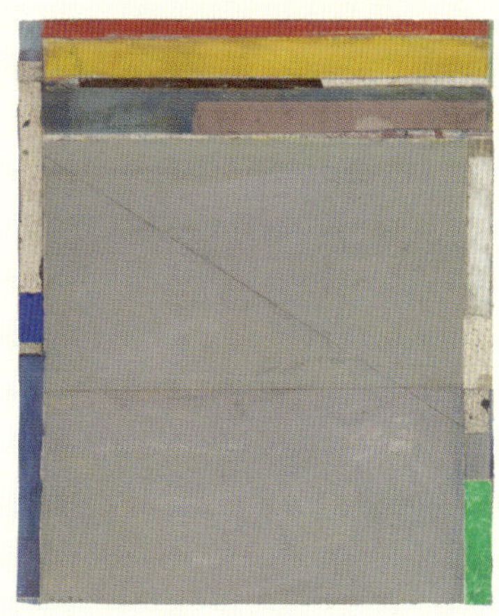

DRAWING FROM OCEAN PARK

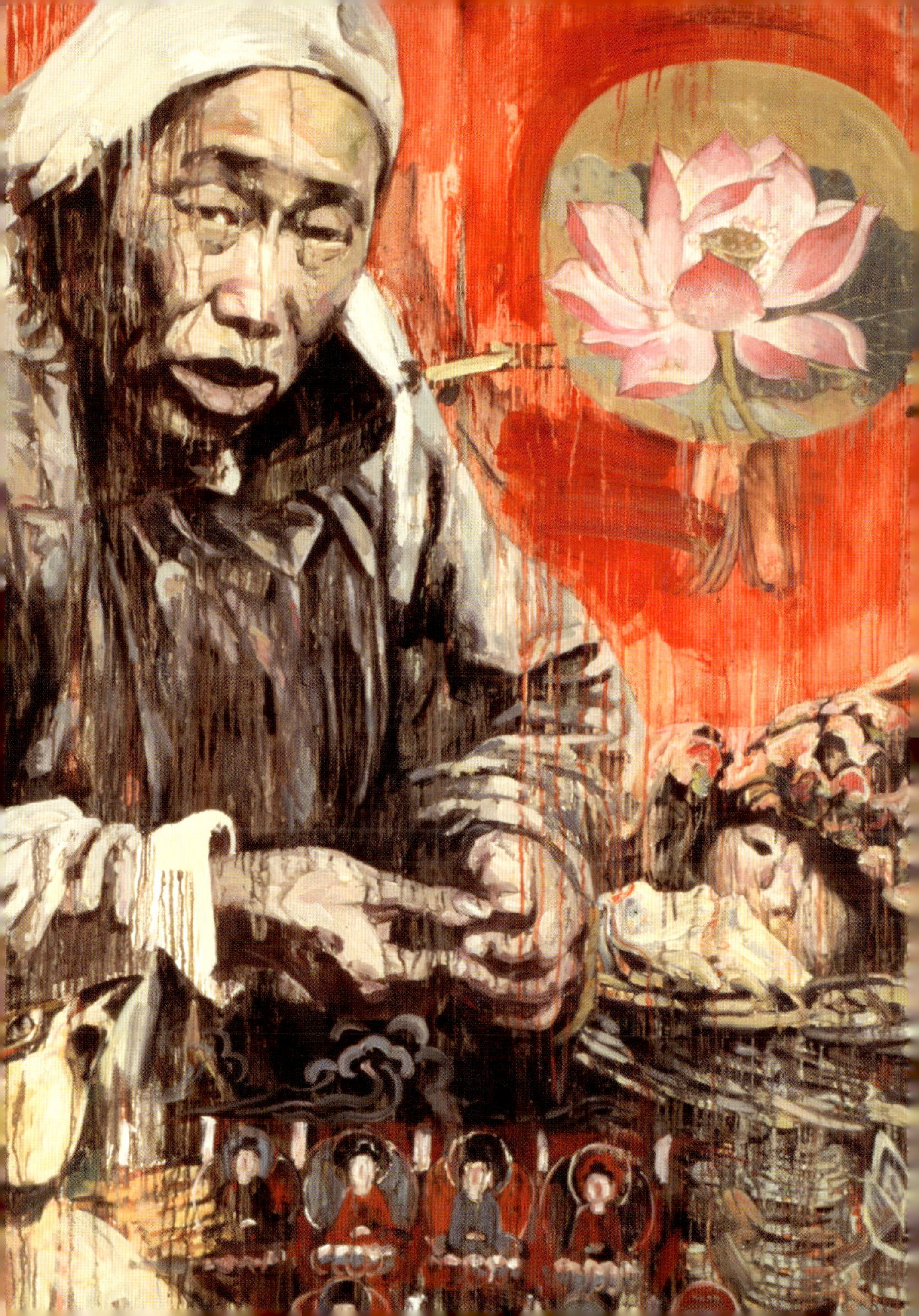

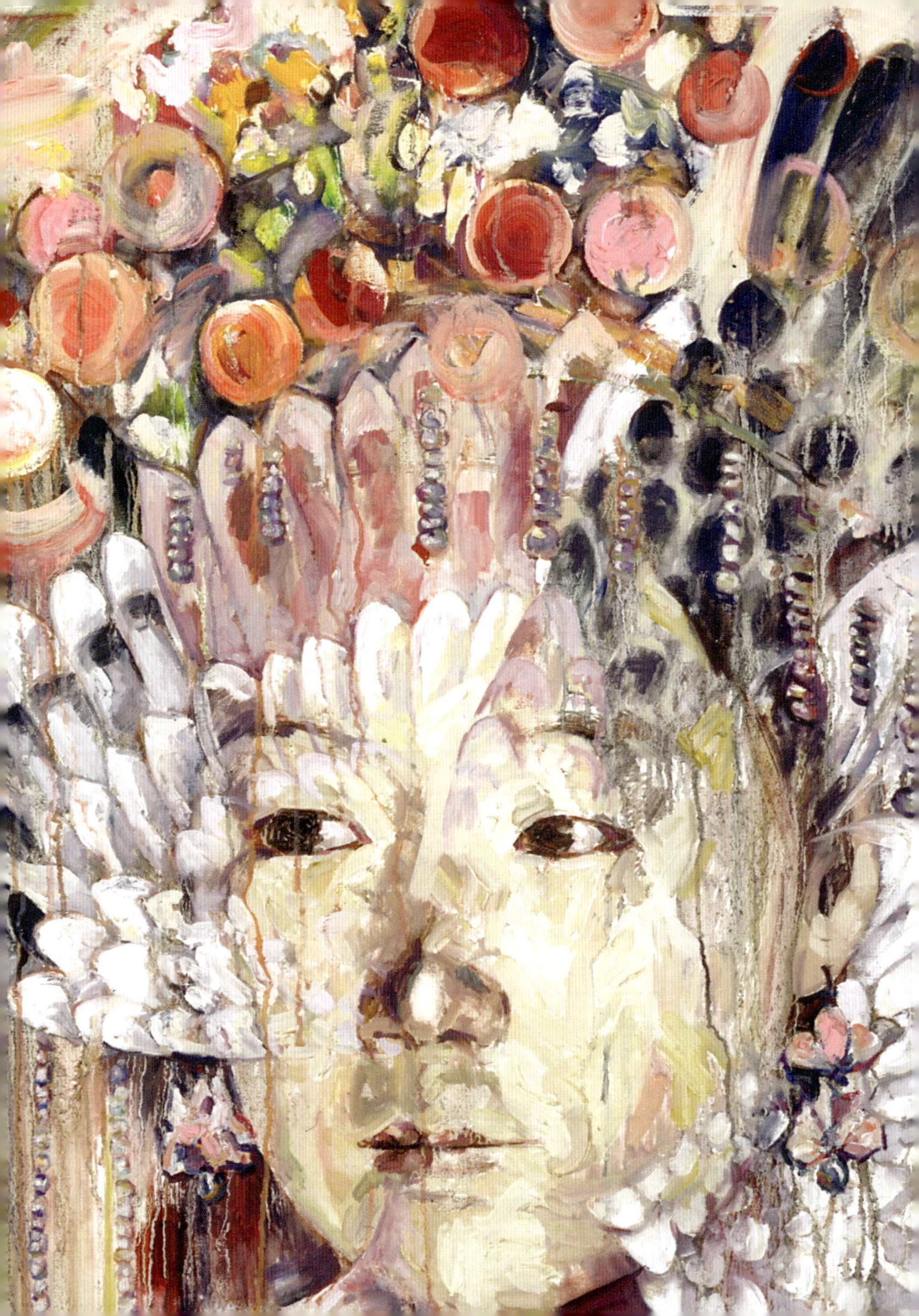